Twayne's English Authors Series

Sylvia E. Bowman, *Editor*

INDIANA UNIVERSITY

P. G. Wodehouse

 44

P. G. Wodehouse

By RICHARD J. VOORHEES

Purdue University

Twayne Publishers, Inc.   ::   New York

To the Memory of My Father and Mother

Preface

In 1956, Herbert Jenkins, Limited, of London, "in response to the requests of many readers," published the first eight volumes of an attractive but inexpensive uniform edition of the books of P. G. Wodehouse. "The intention," said the announcement on the dust jacket, "is to add to this list from time to time until eventually all of the works of P. G. Wodehouse are available in this series." The response of many other readers must have been (as Bertie Wooster would say) to totter and clutch the brow. At the time that the first eight volumes were brought out, Wodehouse had published seventy-eight books. Since then he has published nine more, and a reader might see, in his mind's eye, a race between the uniform edition (called The Autograph Edition because Wodehouse's signature is reproduced on the cover) and the new titles. In his way, Wodehouse is as daemonic a writer as Balzac or Dickens; at the behest of his daemon, he has devoted himself, like Arnold Bennett's Denry Machin, to "the great cause of cheering us all up."

For more than half a century, Wodehouse has served that cause with a popular success for which there are few parallels. The British and American editions and reprintings of Wodehouse's books are so numerous that to catalogue them would be an immense bibliographical task. Moreover, there are translations into all of the major languages of the Western World and into Chinese and Japanese as well.[1] Readers who are familiar with all of the novels and short stories must be rare; but so many people in so many countries know so much Wodehouse, that simply to say that Bertie and Jeeves, Mr. Mulliner and Sir Roderick Glossop are figures in the folklore of the English-speaking world would be to understate the facts. Bertie and Jeeves may be as well-known outside their native country as Sherlock Holmes and Doctor Watson are.

After sixty years, Wodehouse's comedy holds up better than most of Noel Coward's and some of Max Beerbohm's. Wodehouse has an extraordinary verbal exuberance and invention and an inimitable facility for contriving farcical plots and episodes. That he is not a "sophisticated" writer is an advantage as well as a disadvantage. With the passing of a couple of generations, sentimentality does not show through brittleness (if it is there, it is candidly there); audacity does not become dated; urbane posturing is not accompanied by arthritic creaks, as in sophisticated comedy that is not absolutely first-rate. Wodehouse has never tried to be ten minutes in advance of fashion. On the contrary, having been born in the Victorian Age and come to manhood in the Edwardian, he has continued to write as if he were still living in that earlier time. Wodehouse is an innocent, and perhaps it is the obvious kindness, the lack of spite which informs the novels, no less than the wit, that has won him so many readers.

But Wodehouse has only a few critics. Edmund Wilson once said that Dickens did not get the critical attention that he deserved in his own age because his very popularity caused him to be regarded not as a writer, but as an institution. Something of the same thing can probably be said of Wodehouse. In any event, there is only one book on Wodehouse besides this one (and it did not appear until Wodehouse's eightieth birthday), together with half a dozen full-length articles. Fortunately, the quality of most of the writing on Wodehouse is high. I see no need to try to refute much that has been written, but I hope that I have added to a quantitatively inadequate body of criticism.

In the first chapter I recount something of Wodehouse's life as it bears upon his books, for the school years at Dulwich, the brief service in the bank, the residence in the United States, and the work for the theater all illuminate themes, characters, and attitudes in the novels. So do the wartime broadcasts and Wodehouse's other experiences during World War II. Not that the war brought about any change in the novels, for when the war was over, Wodehouse went right on writing the same sort of books that he had always written. Indeed, during the war, when he was interned and imprisoned, he never stopped writing them. But the story of Wodehouse in wartime throws light on the whole of his work.

Preface

The second chapter is a consideration of the public school stories, which, though little known in this country, are still widely read in England. These novels (to be precise, one of the volumes is a collection of short stories) are not without merit in themselves; but a more important reason for considering them is that a vast deal of the characterization, style, and point of view of the mature work is embryonic in the school fiction.

In the third chapter, "Experiments and Transitions," I discuss some early novels that show Wodehouse finding his way out of school fiction and into the kind of adult fiction for which he is best suited, creating a romantic hero but then providing him with a comic Achates, and making a false start in the direction of realism. The fourth and fifth chapters are discussions of the light romantic novels and the comic novels, with some attention given to the developments by which romance becomes a subject for jokes, and melodrama becomes farce. The last two chapters are attempts to describe the Wodehouse world and to place it in the universe of English literature.

I am indebted to Richard Usborne and Wodehouse's other critics for insights, and to Mr. Usborne for biographical information; to the Purdue Research Foundation for a summer grant; to the Interlibrary Loan Staff at Purdue for getting me many books by Wodehouse, and to other Purdue librarians; to J. J. Fettig for loaning me his copies of rare books by Wodehouse; to Helmut E. Gerber for helping me with bibliographical problems; to Mrs. Erling Kildahl for typing the manuscript; to Miss Sylvia Bowman and Frank Kirk for skillful editing.

RICHARD J. VOORHEES

Purdue University

Acknowledgments

I gratefully acknowledge permission to reprint copyrighted material:

From "The Jolly Old World of P. G. Wodehouse." Reprinted by permission of *The South Atlantic Quarterly*.

From the works of P. G. Wodehouse. Reprinted by permission of the author and the author's agents, Scott Meredith Literary Agency, Inc. Also by permission of Herbert Jenkins, Ltd. and A. P. Watt & Son.

Contents

Contents

Chronology

1881 P. G. Wodehouse born October 15, in Guildford, England, the third son of Henry Ernest Wodehouse.

1896–
1900 Educated at Dulwich.

1901–
1902 Clerk in the London Branch of the Honk Kong and Shanghai Bank.

1902 *The Pothunters.*

1903–
1909 On staff of the *Globe.*

1903 *A Prefect's Uncle.*

1903 *Tales of St. Austin's.*

1904 *The Gold Bat.*

1904 *William Tell Told Again.*

1904 First trip to the United States.

1905 *The Head of Kay's.*

1906 *Love Among the Chickens.*

1907 *The White Feather.*

1907 *Not George Washington* (with H. Westbrook).

1908 *By the Way Book* (with H. Westbrook).

1909 Second trip to the United States.

1909 *The Swoop.*

1909 *Mike.*

1910 *Psmith in the City.*

1910 *A Gentleman of Leisure.*

1912 *The Prince and Betty.*

1913 *The Little Nugget.*

1914 Marries Ethel Rowley.

1914 *The Man Upstairs.*

1915 *Something Fresh.*

1915   *Psmith Journalist.*
1917   *The Man with Two Left Feet.*
1917   *Uneasy Money.*
1917   *Piccadilly Jim.*
1919   *My Man Jeeves.*
1919   *A Damsel in Distress.*
1920   *The Coming of Bill.*
1921   *The Indiscretions of Archie.*
1921   *Jill the Reckless.*
1922   *The Clicking of Cuthbert.*
1922   *The Girl on the Boat.*
1922   *The Adventures of Sally.*
1923   *The Inimitable Jeeves.*
1923   *Leave It to Psmith.*
1924   *Ukridge.*
1924   *Bill the Conqueror.*
1925   *Carry on, Jeeves.*
1925   *Sam the Sudden.*
1926   *The Heart of a Goof.*
1927   *The Small Bachelor.*
1927   *Meet Mr. Mulliner.*
1928   *Money for Nothing.*
1929   *Mr. Mulliner Speaking.*
1929   *Summer Lightning.*
1930–
1931   In Hollywood, working for M-G-M.
1931   *Big Money.*
1931   *If I Were You.*
1932   *Doctor Sally.*
1932   *Hot Water.*
1932   *Louder and Funnier.*
1933   *Mulliner Nights.*
1933   *Heavy Weather.*
1934   *Thank You, Jeeves.*
1934   *Right Ho, Jeeves.*
1935   *Enter Psmith* (the second half of *Mike,* published as separate volume).
1935   *Blandings Castle.*
1935   *The Luck of the Bodkins.*

Chronology

1959 *A Few Quick Ones.*
1960 *Jeeves in the Offing.*
1961 B.B.C.'s "Act of Homage and Reparation" to P. G. Wode-
      house broadcast.
1961 *Ice in the Bedroom.*
1963 *Stiff Upper Lip, Jeeves.*
1964 *Frozen Assets.*
1965 *The Brinkmanship of Galahad Threepwood.*

CHAPTER 1

The Life and the Books[1]

I   *Family and School*

DURING a remarkably long and successful career, P. G. Wodehouse has spent a large part of his time making caricatures, hilarious but not unkind, of British institutions and national types. In the works of Wodehouse the London clubs and the stately homes of England, the publishing houses and the law courts, the universities and the Old Vic are populated by an outlandish lot whom he suitably describes as "eggs," "beans," "crumpets," "clothheads," "blisters," "pots of poison," and the like. One gets a hint of their absurdities and imbecilities in a recital of some of their names: Bertie Wooster, Bingo Little, Sir Roderick Glossop, Oofy Prosser, Pongo Twistleton.

In view of his birth and early background, however, the chance that Wodehouse would become a comic novelist and the creator of a fantastic version of British society was the kind of long shot of which even members of the Drones Club would be suspicious. All of the smart money would have been put on the proposition that Pelham Grenville Wodehouse would grow up to be, if not one of the central pillars of the Establishment, at least one of the necessary struts. His father, his three brothers, and two of his uncles spent most of their lives as administrators and educators in Eastern outposts. When he was a boy, it was taken for granted that he would go into the Royal Navy. At his public school he did very well in classical languages, and he was expected to follow an older brother to Oxford. But when the value of the Rupee fell, and with it the value of his father's pension, he went to work in the London office of the Hong Kong and Shanghai Bank. In the normal course of affairs he would have learned the business and then gone out to one of the branches in the East.

Wodehouse was born on October 15, 1881, in Guildford, a town about thirty miles southwest of London. He was the third son of

Henry Ernest Wodehouse, who, in his career in the Hong Kong Civil Service, rose to a judgeship and was made a Companion of the order of St. Michael and St. George. Wodehouse's own time in Hong Kong amounted to only one year, between the ages of two and three, and his parents' leaves to England were infrequent. As a boy, therefore, he spent most of his time, when not in school, with friends and relatives. For a while he lived with people named Prince in Croyden, but he was more often with aunts and uncles. From this circumstance derive two of the major figures and some of the main motifs of Wodehouse's books. The Wodehouse uncle is not cruel, but he is frequently capricious and usually disposed to doubt the earnestness and responsibility of the young. He hesitates to turn over money that he holds in trusts for nephews, wants them to take jobs that are good for their characters but revolting to their tastes, and is insufficiently understanding when they exceed their allowances. The uncle, however, is not often an active evil, and the closest thing to dread that he inspires is a feeling of dependence because he can withhold wealth. But the aunt, probably because aunts are around more of the time, is authority at its most formidable, most constant, and most perverse.

An aunt may be jovial, like Bertie Wooster's Aunt Dahlia, or she may be stern, like his Aunt Agatha (who, Bertie says, eats broken glass and turns into a werewolf when the moon is full). But the essential nature of the aunt is to force on a nephew precisely what he recoils from—and to refuse him precisely what he craves. To improve Bertie's mind and character, Aunt Agatha compels him to go to performances of Shakespeare and Chekhov, and to tour galleries and museums. She drags him with her to dull resorts at the seaside. She assigns him the task of watching over a friend's son, whose main ambition is to stay drunk most of the time. She tries to get him married to a series of dreadful girls. Aunt Dahlia, whose opinion of Bertie's intellect is even lower than that of Aunt Agatha (more than once she has thought of having him certified mad) does not try to reform Bertie. Indeed, she needs reforming herself. Raffish where Agatha is respectable, she blackmails Bertie to speak to grammar-school students on prize days, butter up bores from whom she wants something, and steal silver cream pitchers, paintings, and other valuable objects from country houses.

Life around young Wodehouse's aunts was not, of course, quite as harrowing as life is around Agatha and Dahlia. And even in a world dominated by aunts, there were auntless interludes of great charm. Accompanying his aunts on formal calls, the boy often went to the servants' quarters for tea, and until the moment when the butler came to say that the young gentleman was wanted, he had the time of his life. "My mind today," says Wodehouse, "is fragrant with memories of kindly footmen and vivacious parlormaids." [2] Wodehouse's novels contain enough servants, kindly, vivacious, and otherwise, to staff a dozen Berkley Square mansions and country houses. The calls of his boyhood enabled him to deal with servants, not only in relation to masters and mistresses, but also in relation to one another. A few years after the calls with his aunts, Wodehouse, dressed in clothes borrowed from his brothers or cousins, was himself ringing door bells at five o'clock. This experience is the main reason why the butler in the Wodehouse world is not a servile, but an imperial figure. In his seventies Wodehouse still remembered the appearance of the butler as the door swung open, a man of seventeen stone, with "mauve cheeks, three chins, supercilious lips, and bulging gooseberry eyes that raked you with a forbidding stare. . . ." [3]

Wodehouse's school years were, in some ways, the most important period of his entire life. In this respect he is no more than typical of British writers and of middle- and upper-class Englishmen generally. But his response is not at all typical. The literature of the public school in the twentieth century is voluminous, and most of it is, in some shape or other, critical. The majority of the essays collected and edited by Graham Greene in *The Old School* (1934) are marked, not by gratitude, affection, and nostalgia, but by distaste, disgust, bitterness, and indignation. In another book, *The Lawless Roads* (1939), Greene tells how the school world appeared to him as a Hell, and convinced him of original sin. Reviewing *The Old School,* E. M. Forster complained of its dominant note of shrill hostility, but in his novel *The Longest Journey* (1907), Forster himself provides a damning picture of the public school. The memoirs, essays, and novels of countless other Englishmen are testimonies to their unhappiness at school and protests against the whole system. For a while, the antischool story was as violent as the antiwar story, and some writers, like Richard Aldington in *Death of a Hero,* combined the two. Even so resilient a person as Sir Winston Churchill said that he was happy in the nursery, in the Army, and in politics, but not in school.

For Wodehouse, on the contrary, the school years were sheer bliss. He was to go to Dartmouth (from which young men went into the Navy), but he went to Dulwich instead, because when he visited his brother Armine there he fell in love with the place. He has never fallen out of love with it, and its spell in one way or another is upon all of his books, early and late. Dulwich was founded in 1619 by Edward Alleyn, the Elizabethan actor-manager, as The College of God's Gift. When Wodehouse was there, it was a complex of Victorian brick buildings surrounded by sixty-five acres of fields and woods. Though Dulwich is versatile, having graduated one major philosopher of the twentieth century, one great explorer,[4] eminent statesmen and scientists, and famous cricketers, it has a strong literary and theatrical tradition. A. E. Mason, C. S. Forester, Raymond Chandler, and Leslie Howard all went to Dulwich. The town of Dulwich was not developed beyond the village state until the nineteenth century. (It was to Dulwich that Dickens retired Mr. Pickwick at the end of his adventures.) As a London suburb of sixty thousand, it still retains something of its earlier rural atmosphere. In several of Wodehouse's novels it becomes "Valley Fields," most recently in *The Ice in the Bedroom,* published in 1961.

When Wodehouse arrived at Dulwich, his brother Armine had not yet left. Armine's career had been a distinguished one, and some invidious comparisons were inevitable. For example, Wodehouse's French master (later a professor of French at Cambridge) considered that the younger brother was inferior to the older both in brains and in application. Some of the disadvantages of joining and older brother at school are reflected in the school novel *Mike* (1909).[5] First, Mike does not like being supervised by his brother Bob (for that matter, Bob does not relish the role of supervisor, but his parents expect him to play it). Second, Mike suffers a conflict between ambition and fraternal loyalty. He desperately wants to get a place on the Wrykyn cricket team, but he cannot, in good conscience, do so if he is to replace Bob.

Wodehouse's rivalry with Armine, however, was not so fierce

as Mike's with Bob. Wodehouse was at Dulwich for two years
after Armine left, and he achieved many of the same honors that
Armine had. For one year he played on the first football team,
and for two years he played on the first cricket team. He became
a prefect. He distinguished himself in Latin and Greek composition and wrote verses in the manner of W. S. Gilbert for the
school magazine. He delighted in the camaraderie of school and
formed friendships like the one with William Townend, which
has lasted seventy years. Evidently, school provided the occasion
for all of the pleasures he needed and the opportunity for exercise
of all the talents he possessed at the time. In his later years he
became one of the most faithful of "old boys," and today he is
the president of the Old Alleynian Association of New York.

The years at Dulwich gave Wodehouse the materials for seven
of the first twelve books that he published. As one might expect,
the school novels make the school world a kind of earthly paradise, and most of the boys in them have the wit to see that they
live a privileged life. They feel a proper loyalty and an eagerness
to uphold the name of their school. But one, clearly modeled in
part on Wodehouse himself, feels a passionate gratitude and
enthusiasm. Adair, the captain of cricket at Sedleigh, is an orphan;
his guardian is a gout-ridden old fellow who cannot be much
fun for a boy to be around. As far as Adair can remember, the
only happy times he has had have been at school. He knows that
Sedleigh is not one of the great British schools, but he dreams of
its becoming great, and he devotes himself to making it so. Somewhere in the future he sees "a colossal establishment, a public
school among public schools, a lump of human radium, shooting
out Blues and Balliol Scholars year after year without ceasing." [6]

The school years, however, had more permanent and important
consequences than the school novels or any character in them.
Wodehouse's reading and writing at Dulwich did much to fix the
flavor and shape of all of his books. In the curriculum he read
Shakespeare, Tennyson, and other poets, the quoting of whom was
to become one of the earmarks of his style. Richard Usborne believes that the quotations from Shakespeare are simply those that
any fifteen-year-old boy picks up in class; indeed, Wodehouse is
particularly fond of such scraps as "the poor cat i' the adage"
and "We shall meet at Phillipi." But Usborne may underestimate

Wodehouse's interest in Shakespeare even at school, for a good many less familiar quotations appear in the earliest novels. At school Wodehouse was already an eager reader of Dickens. And William Townend says that Wodehouse introduced him to the later Victorian novelists, the stories of Kipling and Doyle, and the operas of Gilbert and Sullivan. By quotation or otherwise Wodehouse brings all of these to his novels. At Dulwich, Wodehouse also learned to construct the clean English sentence that other writers have admired and which caused Hilaire Belloc to call him the best prose writer of his time. And, having been exposed to Aristophanes, he tried out his comic talents in some plays about boys and masters.

During his school days Wodehouse developed an interest in Dulwich teams and outdoor living that has persisted throughout his life. Between wars he often went to cricket and rugger matches at Dulwich and sometimes wrote them up for *The Old Alleynian*. During World War II, when his own fortunes were in very bad shape, he was delighted to hear that in the previous season's cricket Dulwich had won all of its matches, even those with Malvern and Harrow. Cricket and other sports leave a large mark on the school novels, and on the later fiction as well. First, matches occupy a good proportion of the space in the school stories and usually provide the climaxes. Second, games furnish the main basis of the moral code of the schoolboy. The loyalty to the school and the willingness to think of others first are clearly fixed to the morality of the cricket field. Moreover, the good physical condition required for good cricket is itself a morality. For most boys in the school fiction, the greatest occupation in the world is that of agent on a large estate, where one can work in the open air and play cricket for his county. And when Wodehouse has left the school stories behind him and his heroes are not cricket players but young writers, they are still athletic types who are careful to keep themselves fit.

II *Apprenticeship*

When, instead of going to Oxford, Wodehouse went to work in the London branch of the Hong Kong and Shanghai Bank, he joined an already overstaffed business. For the bank was a "nursery," and a certain number of young men had to learn about banking before they were transferred to Eastern offices, even if there was not enough work to keep them busy. In *Psmith in the City* (1910) the personnel of the New Asiatic Bank take an hour and a half for tea (though a ten-minute sign is posted), read novels behind their ledgers, and drift from one department to another to talk with their friends. But if the job was not arduous, it was a comedown for a young man of Wodehouse's expectations. One of the very few depressing episodes in the whole of Wodehouse occurs when Mike Jackson leaves the glamor, glory, and companionship of school to go to work in the bank and live in a furnished room. Wodehouse does not have the heart to leave Mike in his wretched lodgings. After one night Psmith appears and takes Mike to live with him in his flat. At the close of the book Mike's brother Joe telephones him that the Surrey cricket team is a man short because of injury, and Mike walks right out of the bank to play for his county.

Wodehouse was probably not a very good bank clerk. In the autobiographical *Over Seventy* (1957) he talks about his incompetence in the kind of Robert Benchley vein where the reader assumes that everything is grossly exaggerated. But *Psmith in the City* suggests that young Wodehouse, if he could tell a fixed deposit from an inward bill, could not do much more and did not care to. Mike is equally bored and baffled by the entire business. He has no idea how the departments interlock, no clue why they should even be under the same roof.

Altogether, the bank period was evidently a grim one even for a person of Wodehouse's natural cheerfulness. In *Over Seventy* he can joke about banks, but all through the school novels the mere idea of going into a bank is dreadful. In fact, the threat of a job in a bank is the equivalent of the threat of apprenticeship to a greengrocer in Butler's *The Way of All Flesh*. If a boy misbehaves or loafs and stays in the same form for a couple of years, he is dropped out of school and turned into a bank clerk. A passage in *The Head of Kay's* (1905), describing the fate of one such boy, has a bitterness that is unusual in Wodehouse. The boy "had been snapped up in the middle of the holidays—to his enormous disgust—by a bank, which wanted his services so much that it was prepared to pay him 40 pounds a year simply to enter the addresses of the outgoing letters in a book and post them when he completed the ceremony. After a spell of this he might hope to be transferred to another sphere of bank life and thought, and at the end of his first year he might even hope for a rise in his salary of ten pounds, if his conduct was good, and he had not been late on more than twenty mornings in the year." [7]

His work in the bank did not prevent Wodehouse from embarking on a literary career. During his two years as a clerk, he wrote in the evenings and on weekends. Then, through a former master at Dulwich, he got a job on the *Globe*, London's oldest evening paper; eventually he inherited his old master's *By the Way* column. His work at the newspaper was over at noon, and he had the rest of his time for free-lancing. But the *Globe* salary was not princely; Wodehouse had some precarious intervals. And yet this period of his life was apparently a pretty enjoyable one. In *Something Fresh* (1915), which has young magazine writers for both hero and heroine, Wodehouse speaks of "the Free Masonry among those who live in large cities on small earnings." [8] Living in London, Wodehouse and his old Dulwich friend William Townend exemplified that Free Masonry. Townend's anecdotes about the misadventures of another friend, who tried to start a chicken farm, gave Wodehouse some of the materials for his first non-school novel, *Love Among the Chickens* (1906). Later, Townend supplied Wodehouse with plots for short stories about Ukridge, the bumbling comic hero of *Love Among the Chickens*. In return, Wodehouse staked Townend to a voyage on a tramp steamer which led to his career as a writer of adventure novels.

Wodehouse did a certain amount of outlandish and ill-paid hack work, as recurrent situations in the novels suggest. Bingo Little, Monty Bodkin, and other young fellows serve time on the staffs of such magazines as *Tiny Tots;* Bertie Wooster's Aunt Dahlia is the proprietor of a women's journal called *Milady's Boudoir;* and Joe Vanringham, a professional writer, is involved with the publishing house of the crook, Busby. But Wodehouse learned his trade rapidly. Soon he was not only publishing school serials in the best boys' magazines of the time (*Chums, The Public School Magazine,* and *The Captain*), but also publishing stories in *Strand*. With publication in the latter, he had arrived. This magazine, which began publication in 1891 and ceased in 1950, was one of the earliest and one of the best of the popular monthlies. For *Strand* Arthur Conan Doyle wrote the Sherlock Holmes stories; Kipling, *Puck of Pook's Hill;* and H. G. Wells, *The First Men in the Moon.* Among other contributors were W. W. Jacobs and Denis Mackail. Between 1905 and 1950 *Strand* published most of what Wodehouse wrote.

From the very first, Wodehouse's school serials were good enough to be issued and reissued as books by the firm of A. and C. Black. The *Pothunters* appeared in 1902, when Wodehouse was only twenty-one years old. In the next five years, five other school novels followed, and in 1909 came *Mike,* which George Orwell called the best school story in the language. In 1935 A. and C. Black published the second half of *Mike* (the longest of Wodehouse's books) as *Enter Psmith.* In 1953 Herbert Jenkins reissued *Mike* in two volumes, *Mike at Wrykyn* and *Mike and Psmith.*

III *Journeyman and Master*

In 1904, on his vacation from the *Globe,* Wodehouse sailed to the United States. He liked the country so much that he returned in 1909. This time he brought two short stories with him and sold both of them on the same morning, one to *Cosmopolitan* for two hundred dollars and the other to *Collier's* for three hundred. No British magazine had ever paid him anything like these prices. In consequence, Wodehouse mailed his resignation to the *Globe,* settled down in a room in the Duke Hotel in Greenwich Village, and started to write for the American market. But *Cosmopolitan* and *Collier's* did not take any more short stories from him just then, and for about five years he turned his hand to all sorts of other writing. Under a number of names—P. G. Wodehouse, Pelham Grenville, J. Plum, and so on—he wrote several articles for each issue of *Vanity Fair,* a "smart" magazine, and he was also drama critic on *Vanity Fair.* For pulp magazines, he wrote detective stories.

A turning point in Wodehouse's career came in 1914, when *The Saturday Evening Post* bought *Something Fresh,* the first volume of the Blandings Castle saga. Through the years, the *Post* was Wodehouse's best American customer. Altogether, it published twenty-one of his serials, paying him thirty-five hundred dollars for the first, raising him by stages, and paying him forty thousand dollars for the last twelve. The prestige of the *Post* opened other doors, and Wodehouse wrote again for *Collier's* and *Cosmopolitan,* and started to write for *Redbook, The Woman's Home Companion,* and other popular magazines. The serials were later published as novels, and the short fiction in collections of short stories. Wodehouse enjoyed the rich revenues of the slicks, but his gains were not merely monetary. Always modest enough to take advice, he profited from the criticism of his editors, especially that of George Horace Lorimer, the editor of the *Post,* and his staff. Rewriting and cutting, removing characters and scrapping scenes, he grew in discipline as well as facility.

His eyesight kept Wodehouse out of the British Armed Forces in World War I, and he spent the war years in the United States. While he was writing his third *Post* serial, he took on work in musical comedy, an area which he had very slightly penetrated in London. In 1904, he wrote a lyric for *Sergeant Brue* at the Prince of Wales Theater. In 1906, he got the job of encore-writer for *The Beauty of Bath* at the Aldwych. There he met Jerome Kern, who had come to London hoping for better luck than he had been having in America. Together they wrote a topical song, "Mr. Chamberlain," for Seymour Hicks (later Sir Seymour Hicks). A playwright and author of books on acting and the theater, as well as a singer, comedian, and character actor, Hicks became a friend of Wodehouse. He served as the model for an actor called Higgs in one of Wodehouse's school novels. When, in 1915, Wodehouse and Kern met in New York, they worked with Guy Bolton (who did the books) on a series of musical comedies for the Princess Theater. The second of the "Princess Shows" was an immense success, and from then on any theatrical manager was glad to have the team writing for him. In one season, Wodehouse, Kern, and Bolton had five shows running simultaneously on Broadway, and also had twelve companies on the road. At one time or another, Wodehouse also wrote lyrics for Franz Lehar, Victor Herbert, Sigmund Romberg, Rudolf Friml, George Gershwin, Cole Porter, and half a dozen other composers.

In the 1920's Wodehouse also did a great deal of other work for the stage. He collaborated with Guy Bolton on straight plays, wrote dramatic versions of his own novels, and adapted foreign plays. Ferenc Molnar was so pleased by the adaptation of *The*

Play's the Thing that he wanted no one but Wodehouse to touch his work. Once at the Casino in Cannes he stopped play at one of the tables for five minutes to deliver a speech in praise of Wodehouse's talents. All told, Wodehouse was author or part author of sixteen straight plays, and wrote for John Barrymore, Douglas Fairbanks, Tallulah Bankhead, Gertrude Lawrence, and Leslie Howard.

The history of the musical comedies for the Princess Theater is told in *Bring on the Girls* (1953), written in collaboration with Guy Bolton; further information about Wodehouse's career in the theater is to be found in his autobiographical *Over Seventy* and in the letters to William Townend collected in *Performing Flea* (1953). But the theatrical experiences also went into Wodehouse's novels in several ways. *A Damsel in Distress* (1919) and *Jill the Reckless* (1921), for instance, have show-business backgrounds and make rather full use of Wodehouse's technical knowledge of rehearsals, bills of cost, Equity provisions, and the like. To the Wodehouse world the theater also added new character types like the tough theatrical manager and the brave, cheerful, and chaste chorus girl. Wodehouse used the latter not only in the theater novels but also in the country house novels; introduced into a place like Blandings, she provided valuable contrasts with its permanent residents. Some of the heroes of the novels were, like Wodehouse himself, playwrights or musical comedy writers. Also, the work for the stage influenced the technique of Wodehouse's fiction, strengthening his inclination to emphasize dialogue over narrative and to divide a novel into a series of scenes. The labors in musical comedy had a further influence on Wodehouse by accentuating his tendency to confine his fiction to a world in which the problems of the real world are either absent or solved out of hand.

His fiction selling widely, his services sought for both the London and New York stages, Wodehouse could live and work wherever he wanted to. In 1914 Wodehouse had married Ethel Rowley, the widow of Leonard Rowley of Cheshire. In the 1920's and 1930's the Wodehouses, with their maids, cats, dogs, and birds, were a familiar sight on Atlantic liners and Channel boats, at English estates and French resorts. Wodehouse rented a number of English country houses, and then, in 1934, he bought a house called Lowwood in Le Touquet. Wodehouse met the celebrated writers of the time. Arnold Bennett was amiable but patronizing. Hugh Walpole was jealous of Wodehouse's popularity and of the great compliment paid by Belloc to Wodehouse's style. The first thing that H. G. Wells said was that his father had been a professional cricketer. At the same time Wodehouse became acquainted with British aristocrats and statesmen. (*Carry On, Jeeves,* a book published in 1925, is dedicated to Bernard Le Strange; *Meet Mr. Mulliver,* published two years later, is dedicated to the Earl of Oxford and Asquith.) Wodehouse met Winston Churchill six or seven times, but between times Churchill always forgot who Wodehouse was. Also, Wodehouse met a good many Americans. Accordingly, the backgrounds and casts of the novels were enlarged, and the Wodehouse diction, already a complex amalgam, was given yet another element.

Wodehouse's fame as a writer of light comedy made offers from Hollywood inevitable, and in 1930 he accepted one. Metro-Goldwyn-Mayer paid him handsomely but scrapped almost everything that he wrote for the screen. In the spring of 1931 the studio did not renew his contract. Wodehouse told an interviewer from the Los Angeles *Times* that he had enjoyed his stay in Hollywood, and that he only regretted that he had got so much money for so little work. With this honest and innocent remark, Wodehouse suddenly became an unpopular figure in several quarters. The Anglophobes flew into a passion. The bankers from the East Coast rushed to Hollywood, and a revision in studio policy, no doubt long overdue, took place.

But Wodehouse had made some good friends in Hollywood, for instance, the actress Maureen O'Sullivan, to whom he dedicated *Hot Water* (1932), and her husband John Farrow, the director. Hence he returned to Hollywood to work for RKO in 1936. He was pleased to do the script for one of his own novels, *A Damsel in Distress* (1919) for Fred Astaire and Joan Fontaine, with a score by George Gershwin. (Earlier, RKO had given the book to another screen writer, who had turned it into a gangster drama without the slightest resemblance to the original.) Wodehouse admired the directors for whom he wrote, George Stevens and Edmund Goulding. But he found writing scripts an uncongenial task, and he kept thinking of a novel that he had blocked

out and was eager to write. Fortunately, his final departure from Hollywood was unattended by any commotion.

Hollywood, however, had treated badly the first time—and indifferently the second time—a writer who could have been extremely valuable to the movies. Though Wodehouse made no attempt to get revenge by way of writing an anti-Hollywood novel, he said in one of his wartime broadcasts that being rushed by the Germans from a prison camp to a train and then waiting all day for the train to start reminded him of being in Hollywood. There, too, the procedure of feverish haste followed by endless delay was customary. The Hollywood about which Wodehouse wrote a number of short stories is merely a nominal one, for the stories might just as well have been set somewhere else. To the gallery of characters in his novels, however, Wodehouse added a couple of important ones: Ivor Llewellyn, the producer, and Lottie Blossom, the actress with the floodlight eyes and shattering laugh.

Aside from the intervals in Hollywood, the 1920's and 1930's were great times for Wodehouse. He was doing the work that he wanted to do, and he was getting very well paid for it. During his fifteen most productive years, between the world wars, his annual income was one hundred thousand pounds. The critics, of course, had paid almost no attention to him, but in June of 1939 he received a tribute from the intellectual world, and a major one at that, a Doctor of Letters from Oxford University. Speaking in Latin hexameters, the Public Orator of the University praised Wodehouse for the kindness of his temper, the gaiety of his wit, and the finish of his style. A leading article in the London *Times* endorsed both the degree and the citation. In making Wodehouse a doctor of letters, said the article, Oxford had done not only what was popular, but also what was right.

IV *Under a Cloud*

Thus, in the summer of 1939, Wodehouse was in a position that any writer would have envied. He might have said, quoting (like one of his characters) from Kipling, that he was feeling like the little friend of all the world. During World War II, however, he must have felt like the toad beneath the harrow. Germans imprisoned him, Frenchmen interned him, and Englishmen accused him of collaboration.

Wodehouse's life from 1940 to 1945 needs telling in greater detail than any other part of his life, though it might seem to require only a very summary treatment. Wodehouse's plight during the war was nothing compared to the suffering of millions of other people, let alone the death of millions. And, unlike happier times, the war years did not leave any perceptible mark on his writing. Nonetheless, there are reasons for telling the story here. If what happened during the war did not make a mark on the books, it made one on the man and on the public image of him. A full account of a story, sometimes told in rumors and hints, sometimes deliberately distorted, and widely misunderstood, will do justice to Wodehouse. It will also cast some light on the whole of his writing. And it will provide a curious, though scarcely edifying, footnote to the history of a great war.

Wodehouse's troubles began almost exactly a year after his tribute from Oxford. In the summer of 1940, Wodehouse was living in his house at Le Touquet. As soon as German soldiers appeared in Le Touquet, the British residents supposed that they would be interned. After a couple of weeks, however, they concluded that their internment was not part of the Nazi program. Apparently they would be required only to report daily to the Kommandatur in Paris Plage. But on June 24, when Wodehouse reported as usual, he learned that British citizens were to be interned after all. He was sent back to Le Touquet, accompanied by a soldier, to pack. Into the one suitcase that he was allowed he put (along with clothing, tobacco, scratch pads, and pencils) an Oxford Shakespeare and a "complete" Tennyson, but he forgot his passport. First he was taken to a prison in Loos, a suburb of Lille. Since he had no passport, he might have been kept there indefinitely, had not other British citizens established his identity. As British Civilian Prisoner Number 796, Wodehouse was later taken to Liege Barracks, next to the Citadel of Huy, and finally to a camp at Tost, in Upper Silesia.

After a total of forty-nine weeks Wodehouse was taken from Tost to the Adlon Hotel, in Berlin. On June 26, 1941, he gave an interview to Harry Flannery, the C.B.S. man in Berlin. Between June 26 and July 2 he recorded five talks that were broadcast,

[32]

not over C.B.S., but over the German network. These broadcasts provoked an enormous uproar in England. There were letters to the papers, angry editorials, protests from other writers, and questions in Parliament. The Ministry of Information called in William Connor, the "Cassandra" of the *Daily Mirror*, to attack Wodehouse. On July 15 Connor delivered a talk in which he denounced Wodehouse as a Quisling and a worshipper of Hitler who had betrayed his country in exchange for a comfortable bed in a big hotel.[9] As a result of Connor's talk, certain British libraries withdrew Wodehouse's books from circulation; the B.B.C. put a ban of his lyrics for at least two years; the Beefsteak Club cancelled his membership; still worse, Dulwich struck his name from the rolls. A number of readers suddenly discovered that the novels proved Wodehouse to have been a Fascist even before Hitler. As long as three years after Connor's talk there were demands from members of Parliament that Wodehouse be tried for treason.

Not all Englishmen, however, regarded the broadcasts as treasonable. The novelist Denis Mackail, for instance, listening to the interview with Harry Flannery, was not indignant, but moved. He thought that Wodehouse was funny and also that he was remarkably courageous, for he was evidently making some sort of protest against intolerance. It was in Connor's broadcast that Mackail found cause for indignation. Besides calling Wodehouse a traitor, Connor sneered at his Christian names and described him as a playboy, whereas Wodehouse was one of the most industrious writers in the world.[10] When he was himself a prisoner of the Nazis in Italy, Air-marshal Boyd read the texts of the five broadcasts that Wodehouse had made over the Nazi radio; he thought them anything but treasonable. Indeed, he could not imagine how the Germans had allowed Wodehouse to say what he had said. Either they had more sense of humor than anyone had ever given them credit for, or the talks had somehow slipped by while the censors were asleep. There were passages, he said, about prisoners being transported in cattle trucks, and a section on Loos Prison that ought to have driven the Germans wild. He suspected that by the time he read the broadcasts, Wodehouse had been shot for making them.[11]

All the same, Wodehouse was widely regarded as a traitor. In the last year of the war he had further trouble, this time with the

French, who arrested him shortly after the Liberation of Paris and detained him for some months. In November, 1944, Malcolm Muggeridge, serving as a liaison officer with the French *Services Speciaux,* was told that Wodehouse was living in Paris; instructions had been received to keep an eye on him, and Muggeridge was pleased to perform this duty.[12] The Wodehouses were staying at the Bristol Hotel, and there Muggeridge went to talk to Wodehouse. Among other things, he said that he considered the row over the broadcasts absurd, but that questions would have to be asked to clear up the whole business. In the immediate circumstances (the atmosphere filled with charges and countercharges of collaboration, the mood of vindictiveness), he explained, Wodehouse's position was serious. Muggeridge was quite right. On November 22, Wodehouse was arrested by the French judiciary police in charge of treason and collaboration cases. His arrest was reported to the British Embassy, and a representative of the Home Office flew to Paris. The presence of the Home Office man instantly changed the flavor of the proceedings; the Wodehouses were given beds, and the next day Mrs. Wodehouse was released. Four days after his arrest, however, Wodehouse himself was taken to a hospital outside Paris and kept under guard.

Some of the details of the Wodehouse affair in its French phase are still somewhat obscure. Evidently there was a certain amount of contradiction, indecision, and downright muddle in the handling of it. A British barrister sent over to investigate the case considered that Wodehouse had neither said nor done anything actually treasonable, or even dishonorable. Other British officials, however, continued to interrogate Wodehouse on the minutiae of his actions and motives. Though he was under guard in the hospital, there was apparently some pretense that he was an ordinary patient. Every day his temperature was taken, and every day it was quite normal. In the morning he wrote, and in the evening he played cards with his warders. Malcolm Muggeridge, as well as some of the personnel of the British Embassy, believed that Wodehouse had been put in the hospital by French officials kindly disposed to him so that he might have decent quarters and food, or so that he might be spared prosecution by fanatics.

In any case, Wodehouse was released from the hospital on

March 7, 1945. Muggeridge drove the Wodehouses through a fierce blizzard to Barbizon. For three weeks they stayed there in a freezing hotel; when the hotel was requisitioned by Supreme Headquarters Allied Expeditionary Forces, they went to live with French friends near Hesdin. After living for a couple of years in a series of French hotels and apartments, the Wodehouses sailed to the United States.

V *The Texts of the Broadcasts*

Accusing Wodehouse of treason made about as much sense as accusing him of pornography or witchcraft would have made. In view of all the goings-on, however, it is natural that some people should still wonder what the broadcasts were all about, and that others should simply assume that Wodehouse was a traitor. The big questions, of course, are what did Wodehouse say on the radio and why did he say it? The broadcasts, together with interviews with the press at the time, were misquoted from the first. As recently as 1954 a review of a Wodehouse novel in an American newspaper made reference to the nightmare that followed when Wodehouse appealed to his countrymen to surrender to Hitler.

But as to the C.B.S. broadcast, anyone who wishes to, may read Harry Flannery's account of it in *Assignment to Berlin* (1942). As to the other talks, the full text of them has been published in *Encounter* under the title "The Berlin Broadcasts" (October and November, 1954). In the C.B.S. interview with Harry Flannery, Wodehouse was clearly indiscreet. (On the other hand, the German censors were themselves curiously indiscreet to permit to pass some of the things that Wodehouse said.) Wodehouse said that he did not mind being a prisoner, that he could get along anywhere so long as he had a typewriter, paper, and a room to work in, and that his suite at the Adlon was a nice one. Speaking of the books that he had written in the prison camps, he said that they were not about the war. Plenty of people were writing about the war, and his readers wanted something different. He wondered if the kind of England that he wrote about would survive the war, whether or not England won. He was very much surprised that the German people showed so little interest in the

Russian campaign. Finally, he expressed a wish to go back to the United States, where he had always felt at home and where he hoped that he would continue to be liked.

The five "Berlin Broadcasts" are in the main a mixture of two Wodehouse characteristics: neat, efficient exposition and narration on the one hand, and foolery on the other. Wodehouse begins by correcting the accounts of his internment that had appeared in British and American papers and magazines.[13] (Among other legends, there was one that Wodehouse was giving a party when a messenger roared up on a motorcycle with the news that the Germans would be there in an hour. Wodehouse and his friends just laughed and went on drinking cocktails.) In the first broadcast he also distinguishes between kinds of prison camp (an *Oflag* for military officers, a *Stalag* for non-commissioned officers and privates and an *Ilag* for civilians). In the last part of the talk he describes the journey from Paris Plage to Loos Prison and the prison itself.

In the following broadcasts Wodehouse gives accounts of the other prisons in which he was confined, as well as the trips from one to another. Sometimes he slept in filthy straw on a stone floor, sometimes on makeshift beds without blankets. His food was thin soup and hard bread, ersatz coffee and sausage, and there was never much of it. To spill one's soup was a disaster. Wodehouse was moved from prison to prison in a cattle truck or, if the journey was longer than the average, in a crowded and locked railway train compartment. He not only lived in dirty quarters, but he also was put to work on dirtier jobs. In some camps he had the feeling of being watched constantly. If the jokes were left out, the reader might readily see a similarity between Wodehouse's account of imprisonment and Arthur Koestler's—might recognize, for instance, the connoisseur's inventory of new prison quarters.

Wodehouse does not make the Germans monsters (though he says that in occupied territory the German Army's motto is "What's yours is mine").[14] But he makes them what Bertie Wooster would call "cloth-heads." Instead of demonstrating the famous German thoroughness, they demonstrate that they do not know the first thing about running a prison camp. When Wodehouse, with fifty other men, arrived at Liege Barracks, the Germans had prepared

containing all of the relevant evidence, which he has read several times. Of all the published evidence, however, the report of Harry Flannery is, in its way, the most convincing. For Flannery, unlike Orwell, Muggeridge, and the others mentioned above, disliked Wodehouse—and Mrs. Wodehouse as well. First, he thought that they were too much interested in money and luxury. Wodehouse complained that he had been obliged to travel from prison camp to Berlin on a train, since no car had been available. Mrs. Wodehouse was upset because a trunk with her dinner dresses had not arrived. Second, Flannery claimed that the Wodehouses were, in fact, getting more comforts and luxuries than other people. Wodehouse received so many cigarettes that some of them were given to less fortunate prisoners. From Denmark and the Red Cross Wodehouse got additional food that kept him in good shape. An appearance of illness in one of the photographs taken of him at the time is merely the result of bad focus.

Flannery, however, is just enough to admit that Wodehouse was simply unaware of what was going on and unaware of the implications of the broadcasts. When the Associated Press telephoned the Adlon to ask whether Wodehouse was going to broadcast on the German radio, Wodehouse replied that he was, indeed, going to—and that the reason was that he had been asked. Then he asked Flannery why people kept inquiring about the broadcasts. What was wrong with doing them? Flannery explained that doing anything at all on the Nazi radio (playing the violin, for example) was propaganda, and that the Nazis would make capital of it. It was then that Wodehouse said, "We're not at war with Germany." He also pointed out that his scripts would not be censored, and he concluded by saying that he just could not understand what all of the fuss was about. When Wodehouse and Flannery were planning the C.B.S. broadcast, Flannery proposed to ask Wodehouse what he thought of the Russian campaign. Wodehouse intended to say, "The bigger they are, the harder they fall." [18] But, Flannery protested, he could not say that. Why? Because, predicting a Nazi victory, it would be propaganda or worse. Wodehouse thought for a moment and then said that the idea had never occurred to him.

The attack on Wodehouse by the Ministry of Information was, as George Orwell pointed out, an expedient. British morale at the time depended on the idea that the common people would have to save the country. A democratizing of the social structure was supposedly taking place, or about to take place. And patriotism had come to be associated with a certain amount of left-wing feeling. In these circumstances Wodehouse made a perfect whipping boy. He was a rich man, but not a powerful one. Therefore, he could be attacked as a traitor and pictured as a parasite. Unlike other sorts of rich men, Wodehouse could do nothing by way of retaliation, and there could be no damage to the social structure.

The British people who allowed themselves to be inflamed by Connor's attack did so, Orwell plausibly suggests, because the war had got to a clearly desperate stage. Earlier, the Chamberlain government, the lack of fighting, the peace moves by labor organizations had kept people apathetic. Now the British had suffered a disaster at Dunkirk; France had fallen; the English were alone; and London was being blitzed. At last people knew that they were in a critical situation. Hatred and rumors were part of the very air that they breathed. When a parody of a Jeeves story, written over some such name as P. G. Roadhouse, appeared in an English-language paper circulated by the Germans among British prisoners, Wodehouse was denounced for writing for the Nazis.

VII *Epilogue to the Broadcasts*

The broadcast episode is not deficient in ironies. Though some listeners found the tone of the broadcasts infuriating, the tone was due in part to the fact that Wodehouse had behaved well during his internment and had done so in a typically British way. When, at the age of fifty-nine and after many years of comfortable living, he was put into a prison camp, he did not feel sorry for himself or go to seed. He got along with other prisoners of all classes, helped to keep up their spirits as well as his own, read and wrote as much as he could, and in general made the best of a bad business. In the broadcasts, instead of making a melodrama out of his hardships, he understated them and turned them into comedy. These very virtues were counted against him. Some of his countrymen were not amused when he informed them that his prison in Tost had previously been the local insane asylum; when he said that prison was all right for a visit but that he wouldn't live there if you gave him the place; or when he remarked that if he were ever asked what he did during the war, he would reply that he cleaned out the latrines at Liege Barracks.

The broadcasts may also involve an irony of a much higher caliber. In a letter to William Townend in the spring of 1947, Wodehouse wrote that certain inquiries had turned up the information that all through the war his broadcasts had been used by the United States Army at the Intelligence School at Camp Ritchie as models of anti-Nazi propaganda. Malcolm Muggeridge also asserts that American Intelligence studied Wodehouse's broadcasts as examples of anti-German propaganda under a mask of apparently innocuous japery.

If Wodehouse's broadcasts made no contribution to the cause of the Allies, his books made a small one. The Germans, says Muggeridge, taking Wodehouse's novels to be literal guides to British manners, parachuted an agent, wearing spats, into the Fen country. Dressed thus anachronistically, he was very soon captured. Muggeridge surmises that if he had escaped detection, he would have made his way to London, hoping to find the Drones Club and make himself inconspicuous by throwing bread around the dining room.

In July, 1961, on the twentieth anniversary of Connor's attack, the B.B.C. made a handsome apology to Wodehouse. Evelyn Waugh broadcast "An Act of Homage and Reparation," in which he said that the B.B.C. considered Connor's talk to be unjust and ignoble, that it had been compelled by the Ministry of Information to put Connor on the air, that it had always felt disgust at having anything to do with the affair, and that it repudiated Connor's charges completely. Among other things, Waugh pointed out that Wodehouse had paid for his bed at the Adlon with his European royalties, not by a bargain with the Nazis. Connor preferred to regard Waugh's broadcast as a disservice to Wodehouse and to see Waugh as a ghoulish exhumer of corpses best left alone. Sticking to his wartime guns, he admitted that his attack had been harsh and bitter, but he contended that it had been necessary in one of the harshest and bitterest periods of English history.[19]

VIII *Survival and Revival*

Neither his imprisonment by the Germans nor his detention by the French stopped Wodehouse from writing, though sometimes he had to write in rooms where a couple of dozen men were engaged in other activities—ping-pong games, for instance. Each morning, he tells Townend in one of his letters, he gets about fifty ping-pong balls on the side of the head while he cudgels his brains for the *mot juste*. During his internment and detention he wrote *Money in the Bank* (1946) and about a third of *Full Moon* (1947). By the time the war in Europe was over, he had finished *Full Moon* and gone on to write *Uncle Dynamite* (1948) and *Spring Fever* (1948). He also managed to write ten stories. Between the books that Wodehouse wrote during the war and the ones that he wrote in the security, comfort, and privacy of peacetime, there is no detectable difference.

In spite of his being struck from the rolls of Dulwich, Wodehouse never wavered in his loyalty to the school. Throughout the war he identified himself with Dulwich, thought about its teams and worried about its boys. In December, 1944 he is distressed by a rumor that Billy Griffith has been killed in combat. The rumor is false, but later Wodehouse is in terrible suspense, wondering whether Griffith will play for England in the Test Matches at Lord's. In the winter of 1946, living at St. Germaine-en-Laye, he learns that the Dulwich football team has won the first four of its matches, and he thinks that it may turn out to be one of the great teams, like the one in 1909. Three weeks later Dulwich is still undefeated. Since there are no Sunday papers in St. Germaine-en-Laye, he goes nine miles to Paris for a London *Times*, so that he can read the results of the match with Bedford. These and other letters may remind moviegoers of the two comic Englishmen in Alfred Hitchcock's early masterpiece, *The Lady Vanishes*. Caught in the middle of a throbbing thriller, shot at and shooting back at Fascists, they are concerned only with getting to a cricket match. Unlike Hitchcock's comedians, Wodehouse knows, if he once did not, that there are more important things in the world, but sometimes he has to remind himself of them.

Perhaps the roll calls, lights out, and so on, of the prison camps made Wodehouse think of the routines and disciplines of Dulwich. Certainly the lack of privacy, together with the spirit of camaraderie, brought back memories and attitudes of school days. Like a good schoolboy believing that his school is the best in the country, Wodehouse tells Townend that the men in his prisons were the best in the world. They were always doing things for him: fixing his watch, repairing his bed, massaging his calf when he pulled a tendon. In one letter Wodehouse draws an explicit resemblance between prison camp and school. Bert Haskins, he says, "was a splendid chap, and I was always so sorry that he was not in my dormitory. It's like being in a house at school. In prison camp you don't see much of people who aren't in your dormitory." [20]

By the summer of 1946 Wodehouse's life had brightened a good bit. Though the broadcast affair had not been universally understood and forgiven, Wodehouse had at least ceased to be one of the bad playboys of the Western World. Dulwich had restored his name to the rolls, and his latest books were doing very well. The British edition of *Money in the Bank* had sold twenty-six thousand copies of the first printing, and a second was being prepared. The American edition of *Joy in the Morning* had sold fifteen thousand copies in advance of publication. In August Wodehouse was working on a dramatic version of *Leave It to Psmith* for production in the United States.

But, unable to decide whether they should sell Lowwood or rebuild it and go back to it, the Wodehouses had no real home. When at last they decided to sell the house, they also decided to go to the United States. This decision made good sense in a number of ways. They had always liked living in America, and, as he said on the Flannery broadcast, Wodehouse had long thought of himself as a kind of American citizen. During the time of his worst disgrace over the broadcasts, he had been gratified to receive friendly letters from American readers. When, in the spring of 1947, he arrived in the United States, his meeting with the reporters was a pleasant one. Shortly afterward, he wrote Townend about a man from the newspaper *PM* who had given him and Mrs. Wodehouse a delightful dinner. These events were harbingers of happy years.

There was also one misfortune in store. For some time Wodehouse had been having trouble with his eyes, and as he was do-

ing the dramatization of *Leave It to Psmith*, the trouble advanced
to a graver stage. In the winter of 1949 additional symptoms
(giddiness, buckling of the knees) made it look as if Wodehouse
were suffering from a brain tumor. But none of the appropriate
tests and procedures revealed any sort of pathology. Wodehouse
was more stoical under the circumstances than anyone is obliged
to be, and he was eventually rewarded with a spontaneous recovery.

For five years the Wodehouses lived in the country in the summer and on Park Avenue in the winter. Now American citizens,
they live the year round in a house with twelve acres at Remsen-
burg, Long Island. The events of the war and the illness of the
postwar years have not dampened Wodehouse's spirits or
changed his way of life. Each morning he goes through the "daily
dozen" exercises that he has done since he read about them in an
article by Walter Camp in a 1919 *Collier's*. After a morning's
writing, he lunches and then takes a three-mile walk to the post
office, probably accompanied by one of his dogs. Before dinner he
does some more writing. His eighty-odd years have scarcely reduced the quantity of his production, and clearly they have not
reduced the quality of it. Richard Usborne is probably right to
say that among the ten best of Wodehouse's books, four have appeared since World War II, and that if he had to pick the best
of the lot, he would pick *Joy in the Morning*, published when
Wodehouse was seventy-six. The recent books have more American slang in them than the earlier ones have. But whether or not
the characters speak of "lousing things up" and "getting this show
on the road," they are the same sort of characters as before. And
the country in which they live and move and have their fantastic
being is neither England nor the United States, but one of Wodehouse's invention.

CHAPTER 2

The School Novels[1]

I The Good Old School

ALTHOUGH some of Wodehouse's school novels are still
widely read by British boys and have recently been reprinted, all of them were published before World War I, the first
in 1902 and the last in 1909. In their early editions they are bibliographical curiosities. They were first issued in a series called
Black's Boys' Library by A. and C. Black, the firm that owned the
Encyclopedia Britannica during the last three-quarters of the
nineteenth century and still publishes *Who's Who*. The firm continues to flourish, but Wodehouse is the only one of the contributors to the series whose name the modern reader would recognize.
The others have the highly respectable sound and the initialed
dignity that appear to have been characteristic of popular writers
of the time, but they constitute a roll-call of forgotten authors:
John Finnemore, P. F. Westerman, R. S. Warren Bell, R. A. H.
Goodyear.

As examples of bookmaking, the volumes are in most respects
excellent. They are printed on better paper than any writer is
likely to get today. The type is large and clear, and there is
plenty of white space. The bindings are first-rate, good-looking,
and durable enough to survive many years of library circulation
or borrowing from boy to boy. But the illustrations are atrocious.
Once they must have attracted readers; today they could only
repel or amuse. Whether black and white or in color, they make
the schoolboys look at least thirty years old; one character, who
wears glasses, looks fifty. Not only fashions in drawing, but also
fashions in dress give the boys a formal appearance in the least
formal circumstances. When they are cheering on a runner as
he lunges toward the finish line, when they are painting a statue
in the park with tar, even when they are smashing windows,

their high collars and tight jackets suggest not so much a scene of vigor or violence as a posed picture of a school group.

If the texts were no better than the illustrations, if Wodehouse were another R. A. H. Goodyear, the school novels would have disappeared long ago, together with hundreds of other boys' books of the time. Why, then, should they have gone into large reprintings throughout the 1920's and 1930's? Why should the Mike stories have been reprinted as late as 1953? Why should school novels written in the Edwardian years and based on memories of the late Victorian age have survived the middle of the twentieth century? They are clearly superior to most of the boys' books written at any time, but boys do not always prefer the best books. When *Treasure Island* was running in *Young Folks*, it was not as popular as some of the run-of-the-mill serials that had appeared earlier. To be as widely read by boys as he has been for more than sixty years, Wodehouse not only had to write well. He had to write *for* boys; he had to write, for the most part, within the conventions of public school fiction, and when he departed from the conventions, he had to go carefully.

The ordinary boys' story does not give an objective picture of school. Neither does it turn the school into the Inferno of the propagandist or the looney bin of the comic novelist. Instead, it makes school what boys would like it to be or what they imagine it to be. (In his "Boys' Weeklies," one of the articles collected in his *Dickens, Dali and Others,* George Orwell observes that boys who go to good public schools stop reading public school fiction in magazines like *Gem* and *Magnet* at an earlier age than do boys who go to private schools; and that boys who go to private schools stop earlier than working-class boys who go to a Council school or to none at all.) Since Wodehouse had enjoyed Dulwich immensely and had missed it as much for a year or two after he left, it was natural and easy for him to paint school as better than the rest of life and to make the schools in the novels better than any real school.

In Wodehouse's school novels all of the boys except the bad hats have a satisfying sense of belonging to a group. To be precise, in *The White Feather* (1907) one good boy disgraces himself by running from a fight with town boys and is ostracized by the school; but he is allowed to redeem himself: he takes boxing lessons in secret and at the close of the book wins a match for the school at Aldershot. With the sense of belonging goes a sense of well-being. It may not be so euphoric as the mental atmosphere of the boys' magazines that George Orwell discusses in "Boys' Weeklies," but it is the next thing to it. The mental world of *Gem* and *Magnet*, says Orwell, is rather like this:

The year is 1910—or 1940, but it is all the same. You are at Greyfriars, a rosy-cheeked boy of fourteen in posh tailor-made clothes, sitting down to tea in your study on the Remove passage after an exciting game of football which was won by an odd goal in the last half-minute. There is a cozy fire in the study, and outside the wind is whistling. The ivy clusters thickly round the old grey stones. . . . Lord Mauleverer has just got another fiver and we are all settling down to a tremendous tea of sausages, sardines, crumpets, potted meat, jam and doughnuts. After tea we shall sit round the study fire having a good laugh at Billy Bunter and discussing the team for next week's match against Rookwood.[2]

There is also a great sense of a great tradition. The names on the panels in the Great Hall at Wrykyn, for instance, testify to the many boys who went on to Oxford and Cambridge and to important posts in the Indian Civil Service. No less important, the literature of cricket over the years records the names of boys who went on to become famous bowlers or batters. Further, there is an awareness that the school is in many ways a private world privileged to run by its own rules and customs. Through the prefect system the boys themselves see to discipline up to a point. Masters sometimes have to punish boys, but they will also protect them from the outside world. Indeed, there is an expectation of certain extraterritorial rights in the towns that lie near the school.

The awareness of belonging to the school, of having custody of its reputation and title to its traditions, begets a very comfortable snobbery. In the school stories the school servants play as small a part as servants do in the novels of Jane Austen. When they have any lines at all, they speak like cockneys out of Dickens or peasants out of Hardy. "Mr. Gethryn, 'e's gorn out onto the field. . . . 'E come 'arf an hour ago," [3] a knife-and-boot boy replies to a question from one of the schoolboys, whose speech is fluent and impeccable. "Just a-coming in now zur," [4] says a railway porter to another boy of seventeen. As for the working classes generally in the towns near the schools, they appear to work too little and drink too much, especially on payday. The town of Wrykyn swarms with "gangs of youths" who evidently do not work at all, but spend their time "prowling about and indulging in a mild, brainless, rural type of hooliganism." [5] The schoolboys regard these fellows with such contempt as an Oxford man regards a "bargee." At Ripton the boys would prefer to have no support at all for their teams than to have that of the town boys, cheering from outside the fence.

For that matter, the school is pretty supercilious about anybody outside the fence, regardless of occupation, age, wealth, rank, or authority. In *The Head of Kay's* (1905) one boy says that he suspects the Eckleton police of being "pretty average-sized rotters." [6] In *Mike* (1909) one policeman is not a rotter, but he is clearly a Keystone Cop. Caught in a brawl between schoolboys and town boys, he gets pitched into a muddy pond, his fate foreshadowing that of many policemen in Wodehouse. The Scotland Yard man who appears in *The Pothunters* (1902), as though the theft of a few athletic trophies were of enormous significance, is a Dickensian comic figure. Talking rather like Mr. Jingle, he tells how he recommended a course of flogging for a schoolboy who stole, but recommended clemency for a local poacher and porch-climber. Whatever may be said in its favor, Scotland Yard apparently has some unaccountable prejudice in favor of the lower orders.

At Wrykyn the boys do not think much of the Mayor of the town. When he is not careful, the Mayor drops his aitches, and by way of compensation he speaks in an elaborate and pedantic syntax. Even the nobleman, who, in the persons of such characters as Lords Emsworth and Marshmorton, becomes such an amiable figure in the later novels, may be beyond the pale in the school novels. Sir Alfred Venner is coarse and dictatorial and evidently employs a platoon of gamekeepers to chase boys off his estate. More faithful to the text than most, an illustration in *The Pothunters* depicts him as a bloated monster.

II *Discipline and the Code*

The system of discipline in the school is acceptable because those who administer it are usually intelligent and fair. Speaking of the good judgment of one headmaster, Wodehouse remarks that most headmasters are, in fact, good judges of character. Certainly there is no headmaster in Wodehouse who even remotely resembles Butler's Doctor Skinner, much less the more vicious types of later writers. (Wodehouse's first school novel was published a year before *The Way of All Flesh* [1903] was published posthumously and stimulated the twentieth-century attack on the schools.) There are more good housemasters and form masters than bad ones, but since the risk at this level of personnel is greater, Wodehouse defines the good master with some explicitness. Indeed, he is much more didactic about this than he is about definitions of good boys. Though the specifications are mainly the kind that a boy would endorse, they do not forbid a master to be firm; they only require that he be just. If he is a good athlete, the housemaster coaches his house, and if he is not, he watches games, umpires cricket, and referees football. But a form master who is "thrilled" by a boy's fine cricket will give the boy a bad report if he deserves it, even though the consequence is that the boy will not be allowed to play any cricket at all for some time.

The vices of the bad master are all pre-Freudian. Nothing could be further from Wodehouse's school novels than sadism or the other sinister possibilities of a boarding-school community, even in unconscious forms. Next to injustice, the big fault is fussiness, treating the boys as if they were still in preparatory school. One officious master gets into Wrykyn and gives the impression that he imagines it his duty to carry on a continual warfare against his house. "Mr. Dexter," says Wodehouse, "belonged to a type of master almost unknown at a public school—the usher type. In a private school he might have passed. At Wrykyn he was out of place." [7] The bad master, in short, is not a threat to the persons or the psyches of the boys, but only an irritant to their *amour-propre* and their snobbish sense of seemliness.

Mr. Dexter would no doubt agree with Dickens' Mr. Jaggers that boys are a bad lot. Wodehouse says, in effect, that boys are generally decent and that the key to discipline lies with those boys who are prefects. If they respect their masters, they will see that the rest of the school behaves properly. A prefect is rather like an officer in a military organization, a person with definite privileges and responsibilities and a person about whom a num-

ber of things are simply assumed. In some matters the prefect is
almost above suspicion. When, in *The Pothunters,* the cups are
stolen from the cricket pavilion, the headmaster considers that it
is most unlikely that any public school boy would do such a thing
—and unthinkable that a prefect would. As it turns out, the headmaster is quite right about this case at least. Since his honor is virtually taken for granted, the prefect need not account for his time
or explain his absences as other boys must do. So sacred is this right
that he may absent himself from a cricket match or even quit
play in the middle of one without giving reasons at the time or at
a later date.

Prefects justify their privileges by their competence. A good
headmaster can depend upon them to complete missions just
as a commanding officer depends upon his subordinates. In one
of the novels a boy is lost, but neither the headmaster nor any
other master leads the search for him. Instead, they give the prefects their orders and provide them with the necessary equipment, leaving it to the prefects themselves to organize the rest of
the school into searching parties. Like military officers, the prefects also have powers of reward and punishment. Singly and as
a body, they can give leave to go to town or restrict to school.
They can even inflict corporal punishment. Though Wodehouse
is one of the least cruel of writers, he sees nothing harsh in half a
dozen whacks with a riding crop. As to the possible sexual significance of flogging, it does not enter his mind.

Wodehouse's schoolboys are normal enough to require an occasional rag or row to prevent tedium, but the notion of discipline is so much a part of them that they can behave well in the
absence of both masters and prefects. The most massive defiance
of authority in the school novels is itself an impressive demonstra-
tion of order. Because of a rumpus in the town the Head of
Wrykyn revokes a holiday scheduled to celebrate the recovery
from illness of a member of the Royal Family. In protest, all but
the prefects and the sixth form walk out. But there is no rioting,
because the boy who has conceived the walkout has declared a
species of martial law. The school band accompanies the column.
At an inn some distance from the school, the boy in charge creates
a sensation by ordering dinner for five hundred and fifty. The
newspapers, taking the walkout and "the great picnic" to be an

officially inspired expression of loyalty, warmly praise both the headmaster and the boys.

The public school code, a set of curiously arbitrary rules, has to do with discipline, together with a certain conception of propriety and an image of the ideal schoolboy. According to the code, a boy may not lie directly, except on behalf of others and then in very special circumstances; but so long as he keeps to the letter of the truth, the essence of it is someone else's worry. A boy named Trevor tells the Mayor of Wrykyn that he did not lose his gold bat (a team trophy in the shape of a miniature cricket bat) and that it was in a drawer most of the term. So far as he goes, he is speaking quite truthfully. But the facts are that a friend of Trevor's lost the bat and that it was not in Trevor's drawer most of the term, but in that of an enemy. The case is just what the Mayor has thought it to be all along. The bat was lost, it was lost by a schoolboy, and the Mayor's statue in the town park was painted with tar by that same schoolboy.

The code declares, in effect, that confidence is a virtue but that modesty is a grace that must accompany it. When Mike first comes to Wrykyn, one of the older boys, having discovered that Mike is one of the famous cricket-playing Jacksons, questions him about his record. The dialogue reads like something out of *Alibi Ike*.

"I played a bit at my last school. Only a kids' school, you know," added Mike modestly.

"Make any runs? What was your best score?"

"Hundred and twenty-three," said Mike awkwardly. "It was only against kids, you know." He was in terror lest he should seem to be bragging.

"That's pretty useful. Any more centuries?"

"Yes," said Mike, shuffling.

"How many?"

"Seven altogether. You know, it was really awfully rotten bowling. . . ." [8]

The most important articles of the code concern games. The code prescribes that a boy must prefer games to books or to any other activity, and games in turn teach the code. A boy who reads Herodotus in the original for pleasure, sneers at cricket and football, and decorates his study with china ornaments instead of with sports equipment had better be watched. He is an unsympathetic figure at best, and probably a sinister influence in the school.

For games, first of all, make for house and school spirit. If a house goes season after season without winning a match, it is a total loss. The "slack sheep" are just about as bad as the "black sheep"—no good for games and no good for work, either. In games a boy learns the value of playing as part of a coherent body, not as a random collection of units. This is a lesson that Mike, who even in his early teens shows that he is going to be the greatest of the Jacksons, learns in the second of the Mike novels. Because Mike has not studied enough at Wrykyn, his father transfers him to Sedleigh, which has a reputation for making boys work. At Sedleigh he meets Psmith, whose father has transferred him from Eton for the same reason. Mike and Psmith decide that they will get some of their own back by ragging as much as they can and refusing to play games. In a practice game, however, Mike reveals himself to be a superb cricketer, and Adair, a captain so keen that he will fight anyone who is not, makes Mike fight him. Mike wins by a knockout but, thinking the matter over later, he decides that he likes Adair and that Adair's point of view is the right one.

Second, games teach responsibility on the one hand and obedience on the other. Wodehouse admired *Stalky and Co.* (1899), Kipling's book about public school, but Kipling could not change Wodehouse's views of the uses of cricket and football. In some well-known lines of verse, Kipling spoke of the flanneled fool at the wicket and the muddied oaf at the goal. In *Stalky and Co.* his point is that it is not the teamwork of games that produces strong administrators and resourceful soldiers, but the private enterprise of ragging and rule-breaking. Wodehouse, however, holds to the traditional playing fields of Eton and Battle of Waterloo idea. From his friend Wyatt, by no means a stuffy boy, Mike learns obedience in terms of the cricket field. When the captain of the team orders an early fielding practice, Mike does not show up, because he knows that he is already better than the rest of the team would be if they practiced before breakfast for the rest of their days. But Wyatt explains to Mike: "There are some things you simply can't do; and one of them is cutting a thing when you're put down for it. It doesn't matter who it is puts you down.

If he's captain, you've got to obey him. . . . You'll see that there are two sorts of discipline at school. One you can break if you feel like taking the risk; the other you mustn't ever break." [9]

As for the captain himself, he learns the responsibilities, the scruples, and the anguish of command, the stakes in a game appearing just as important to him as greater ones will appear later in life. He learns, for example, that a captain, as captain, can have no friends. In *The Gold Bat* the captain of cricket will not be bluffed by the secret "League," which demands that he make certain switches on the team. But then the "League" gets hold of his gold bat, which his friend O'Hara has dropped at the foot of the Mayor's statue, and writes the captain a blackmail letter. Now the captain recognizes that, if the alternative is weakening the team, O'Hara will have to confess that he (not the captain) lost the bat, and thus confess that he tarred the Mayor's statue. If a captain can have no friends, neither can he have any enemies. He must put the best man on the team, even though he hates him above all the other boys. To the paramount importance of the team, the family is, however, an exception. Thus, in *A Prefect's Uncle* (1903), the prefect walks out in the interval of a house match to bring back the young uncle, who has gotten into an idiotic scrape and run away from school.

Finally, games teach physical fitness. In the later novels phrases like "bronzed and fit" are among Wodehouse's favorite ironical clichés, but in the school novels such expressions are perfectly serious, and training is something that one does in deadly earnestness. To be sure, one boy overdoes it, and Wodehouse's description of him makes him sound like an earlier version of Anthony Powell's clown, Widmerpool. "Robinson was supposed by many (including himself) to be a very warm man for the Junior Quarter. . . . Being a wise youth, however, and knowing that the best of runners may fail through under-training, he had for the last week or so been going in for a steady course of over-training, getting up in the small hours and going for spins around the track on a glass of milk and a piece of bread. Master R. Robinson was nothing if not thorough in matters of this kind." [10] At the same time Wodehouse can say of another boy, without irony, "He was one of those conscientious people who train in the holidays." [11]

It is because of its effects on fitness, and thus on games, that smoking cigarettes is such a serious offense at school. The penalty for smoking is expulsion, whereas that for playing billiards at public houses, an activity with far more sinful connotations, is merely flogging. But smoking is harmful to a boy's lungs and eyes. There is also a positive side to the non-smoking business. To refrain from smoking is not only an obligation of youth, but also a privilege. If men smoke, they do nothing immoral, but they betray the deterioration that comes with age. Mike Jackson can stride through the world straight, deep-chested, and clear-eyed, but an old wreck like his Uncle John (who is probably all of forty) needs his pipe as a crutch.

III *Soaring Human Boys*

Fortunately for the schoolboys, their inclinations coincide pretty well with the provisions of the code. Their chief interest is cricket, which they will play at any time, in any place, and with any sort of equipment. For instance, two boys on detention dig up a scrap of wood from a cupboard for a bat and roll up a handkerchief for a ball. Cricket, however, is more than a game. It is also a religion. It has its sacred writings: *Wisden Cricketers' Almanack* (usually called *Wisden*), an annual handbook since 1864. This book records scores and averages and includes summaries of all important public-school and second-class county matches, together with longer descriptions of all first-class matches. Cricket also has its rituals for the faithful. Perhaps the most important ceremony in all of the novels is going out at the eleven o'clock interval to inspect the cricket pitch before a big match.

The game also enables the boys to enjoy an esthetic experience without feeling soppy. At Wrykyn the boys all say that their cricket ground is the prettiest in England; it probably has the best view, since one can see three counties from the pavilion. As for the player, especially in an important match, he combines something of the priest with something of the actor or the artist, a feeling of expectancy and isolation before the game, a tension that wears off only in the afternoon innings. Played simply as a pastime, cricket is a better medicine than anything in the pharmacopoeia. In *The Head of Kay's*, one boy, driven to distraction by one of the few bad masters in the novels, consoles himself with the thought that two months' holiday, "with plenty of cricket, would brace him up for another term." [12]

In the Jackson family, with its five brothers, the devotion to cricket is most intense. All of the boys are natural players (Mike has great style long before he has any great strength), and their father hires a professional to coach them during the holidays. Mike plays at his preparatory school, and when he goes to Wrykyn he expects to get into the third "eleven" at the same time that his older brother Bob gets into the first. The three other brothers are already playing for county teams. By the time Mike transfers from Wrykyn to Sedleigh, Bob is playing for Oxford. Even the girls in the Jackson family are cricket buffs. When Mike is at home, his younger sister, Marjorie, fields for him, and she regularly fights with still younger girls over each issue of *The Sportsman*. Mrs. Jackson says almost nothing on the subject of cricket, but it apparently has her tacit approval. If not, she must feel surrounded by monomaniacs.

The boys rather enjoy ragging a few masters in a mild sort of way, though their concentration on games uses up most of the energy that might go into ragging. At Wrykyn a traditional gambit is to make a noise like a cat and then, when the master tells them to stop that noise, to ask, "What kind of noise, Sir?" The hope is that the master will fall into the trap, answer, "This kind," and mew like a cat.[13] In *The Head of Kay's* the boys confine their ragging to the mathematics master. They like to ask him how the great globe was got into the room. Does it come apart, were the walls removed, and so on. In *Mike at Wrykyn* only one short chapter is taken up with this sort of thing. Entitled "The Fire Brigade Meeting," the chapter begins with the boys asking whether they may have uniforms. When uniforms are denied them, they ask whether they may have helmets to protect them from the hazards of fire-fighting. No helmets, either, says the master:

> "Oo-oo-oo-oo-, sir-r-r."
> "But sir, the danger!"
> "Please, sir, the falling timbers!" [14]

There are almost no acts of violence, though there are some dreams of violence. The fire brigade, for instance, is popular because in case of fire it might have to break a few windows and hose water into the masters' studies.

Everything said so far suggests an anti-intellectualism on the part of the boys, and Wodehouse appears to put the seal upon it. In one of the novels a headmaster who cannot sleep gets up and writes an article on the Doxology for one of the reviews. The article, says Wodehouse, served its purpose by enabling the headmaster to go to sleep, but it was rejected, which goes to show the kindliness of Providence. Actually, there is a strong literary strain both in the books and in the boys. Some of the best athletes have already got university scholarships, and all of them read at least some sort of literature for the fun of it. Even O'Hara, whose passion is boxing, reads Hornung's *Amateur Cracksman* when he gets himself thrown out of class. Among the boys' favorite writers is Arthur Conan Doyle. There are frequent references to Rodney Stone, and two of the younger boys name a couple of pet ferrets Sir Nigel (from *The White Company*) and Sherlock Holmes. Sitting in their study, two boys start to translate Livy, but then they break off to talk about the football team. Next they take up the books that they are reading for pleasure. One boy finishes "The Adventure of the Speckled Band" and suggests a stroll before lockup, but the other declines because he is in the middle of *Great Expectations*. The interest in reading is spontaneous, catholic, and undiscriminating—a healthy and honest boys' interest. The same bookshelf that contains Shakespeare also contains *Vice Versa* and *The Rogue's March*.

The results of the miscellaneous reading appear in the conversation of some of the boys, which is as superior to that of the average real boy as their cricket is. Not, of course, on the level of wit and humor that it will reach in the later novels, the talk is still comparatively sophisticated. Mike's friend Wyatt likes to break out at night and shoot at stray cats with an air rifle. (Even if he hits them, he says, it does not hurt them but only stimulates them.) Removing the bars of the window to go on one of his expeditions, he tells Mike that shooting cats is "society's latest craze." [15] In the very first book the boy Charteris says to another who is getting ready for the mile race, "And you'll write to us sometimes . . . and always wear flannel next your skin, my dear boy?" [16] From the beginning Wodehouse also endows the boys with his own habit of quotation and allusion. In all sorts of situations they describe themselves and one another with bits and pieces of Shakespeare, Dickens, Gilbert, Kipling, and many other writers. They stand in doorways like Patience on a monument, resolve never to desert Mr. Micawber, call upon each other to give artistic versimilitude to a bald and unconvincing narrative, and (when locked out of school, for instance) feel like toads beneath the harrow.

Some of the boys not only read but write, and in *The Pot-hunters* Charteris publishes an unofficial monthly magazine. Charteris, whose athletic skills are no more than respectable, is one of the most popular boys in the school; moreover, in his capacities as writer and editor, he is one of the heroes of the book. Besides the mystery of the stolen trophies, *The Pothunters* has a second plot about the plight in which a boy named Jim finds himself. At the start of the book he loses a bet on a boxing match at Aldershot. It was wrong, of course, to bet in the first place, and now he cannot pay. However, he will be able to pay if he wins the mile race, for his delighted father will reward him with more money than he owes. But he loses the race. It looks as if his misdemeanor will be exposed, and he is saved only by an inspiration of Charteris: the profits from a special number of the magazine will cover Jim's debt. So Charteris and his staff stay up all night writing and jelly-graphing the issue. They drink strong tea for a stimulant and feel ever so romantic.

IV *Weaknesses and Strengths of the School Novels*

It is inevitable that in many ways the novels should be no better than any other public-school stories for boys. Some weaknesses follow from the great emphasis on games. First, there are interminable conversations about the comparative strength and skill of various boys on various teams. In the school world a twisted ankle is a tragedy because it keeps a player out of a match. Second, and worse, there are overlong accounts of races and games. The first chapter of *The Pothunters* is taken up with descriptions of boxing matches; Chapter XI is the story of a track and field meet; and Chapter XIV is a sufficiently long recital of a cross-country race. Chapter XVII is rather a relief, for the sport in which the boys engage is at least one without quarters or innings. Looking for a lost boy, they run around in the night in a sort of Robert Louis Stevenson atmosphere, being permitted to carry dark lanterns, trespass on a nearby estate, and shout all over the countryside to the object of their search.

Most of the school novels that follow *The Pothunters* make still more use of games; indeed, games not only take up more space, but also are more closely integrated with the structure of the novels. In *The Head of Kay's* the last two chapters are "The House-Matches" and "The Sports." Several sections of *A Prefect's Uncle* are taken up with cricket matches, and the last section with a football match. *The Gold Bat* opens with talk of a football match and closes with the playing of one. But the stories about Mike Jackson break all records. In *Mike at Wrykyn* there are accounts of practice matches as well as school and county matches, an important match in the middle section of the book, and a more important one in the two chapters before the last. The final chapter, like the first, is a scene at the breakfast table in the Jackson home, where cricket is inevitably the main topic of conversation.

The accounts of the games take up space that the conflict, suspense, and reverses of a proper plot should occupy. In *The Pothunters* the boys pursue the mystery of the stolen cups only when they can take time off from sports. They find the cups by pure accident, and they never find the thief at all. To discover the culprit is the function of the Scotland Yard man, who does so abruptly and without brilliance. He sees a local poacher coming out of a pub with more money than he could have come by honestly. Naturally surprised, he questions the fellow, who becomes frightened and confesses all. In *The Gold Bat* the mystery business amounts to more and is better handled. Who are "The League"? Who wrecked several of the boys' studies? Who tarred the Mayor's statue? These are questions integral to the rest of the action. The reader knows the answer to the last question, but will the officials in the school and the city find it out? Only in the last of the school novels, however, are there hints of the marvelous invention and intrigue that are typical of Wodehouse's later novels. In *Mike and Psmith*, Psmith and a housemaster go through an extraordinary series of moves and countermoves, the master attempting to get hold of a paint-spattered shoe that will convict

Mike of several crimes, and Psmith endeavoring (successfully) to conceal it.

The endings of the school novels are as happy as convention demands, the distributions of rewards and punishments as over-simplified and explicit. The right teams win all or most of the matches, and the good boys go to box or fence at Aldershot. The good characters can also look forward to positions on next year's teams, but the bad ones will not even return to the school, having been dismissed for smoking, transferred to another school, or shoved into a London bank. In *The Head of Kay's* even a bad master is disposed of. He leaves to become headmaster of a plebeian school in the North.

Altogether, the boys at Wrykyn, Sedleigh, and the other schools appear to be satisfied with very little. At the end of *Mike at Wrykyn*, Mike receives a letter from his old school friend Wyatt, who has been saved from a London office and sent out to the Argentine by Mike's father. Wyatt tells how he was wounded (though not gravely) when he shot it out with a trespassing, wire-cutting gaucho on the Jackson ranches, and Mike, pleased that his friend is having such an exciting life, says: "It must be almost as decent as Wrykyn out there." [17]

But boys are, in point of fact, enormously awed by some pretty insignificant matters. Even so bright a boy as Anthony Powell must have been, was curiously susceptible to trifles. Looking out the window on his first morning at Eton, he beheld in the street below a boy of fifteen in the very short trousers, light-colored socks, and top hat customary at the school. His hat far back on his head, one shoulder higher than the other, his knees sagging slightly in the Eton manner, the boy slouched along, whistling a song then very popular:

> K-K-K-Katie, beautiful Katie,
> You're the only g-g-g-g-girl that I adore;
> When the m-m-m-moon shines
> On the c-c-c-cowshed,
> I'll be waiting at the k-k-k-kitchen door.[18]

Powell thought that he had never seen and heard anything so sophisticated in all of his fourteen years, and this initial impression of worldly elegance imparted to him a notion of the school that he never entirely lost. Moreover, Powell in his maturity recalled, with great pleasure, many a schoolboy experience of no spectacular nature: going to an in-bounds pub, sneaking out to an out-of-bounds movie house, playing poker in the matron's room, going up the river to Queen's Eyot for tea and lying in the sun, smoking an occasional cigarette in a ditch, drinking a glass of wine, and so on.

Conventional specimens of school fiction though they are in many ways, Wodehouse's school novels are vastly superior to ordinary school fiction in other ways. If Mike is unaware of the irony of his remark about life in the Argentine and life at school, Wodehouse is not, and in other novels the departures from convention are bolder. In *A Prefect's Uncle* Wodehouse makes a joke of the sacred office of the prefect, the decorum and modesty proper to a new boy, and the dignity proper to an old one. The prefect's uncle, a boy younger than the prefect, and bumptious enough for a dozen, is joined by a boy cut from the same cloth as himself, and both are preceded by letters from aunts that request the older boys to look after them.

In the same book Wodehouse even jokes at those who (like himself) take a passionate interest in cricket. The following passage might well have come, not out of a school novel, but out of one of the comic novels. The superb playing in the match against Pudford, says Wodehouse, "was for many a day the sole topic of conversation over the evening pewter at the Little Bindlebury Arms. A non-enthusiast who tried on one occasion to introduce the topic of Farmer Giles's grey pig, found himself the most unpopular man in the village." [19] Wodehouse goes even further and puts a comic batter in a crucial game with an adult team. Formidable as well as funny, this player drives a ball into the ropes and then congratulates himself: "Rather a nice one, that. Eh, what? Yes. Got it just on the right place. Not a bad bat, this, is it? What? Yes. One of Slogsbury and Whangham's Sussex Spankers, don't you know. Chose it myself. Had it in pickle all winter. Yes." [20]

Sometimes Wodehouse takes a point of view entirely outside the boys' world and makes wholly adult jokes. When the headmaster in *A Prefect's Uncle* discovers that a boy has cribbed an entire poem for a poetry contest, he remarks that plagiarism of this description should be confined to the school magazine and not be permitted to spread to poetry prizes. Even some of the boys themselves have already acquired the adult detachment, the amiable cynicism of the headmaster. "When we get licked tomorrow by half-a-dozen wickets," said Jimmy Silver, tilting his chair until the back touched the wall, "don't say I didn't warn you. If you fellows take down what I say from time to time in notebooks, as you ought to do, you'll remember that I offered to give anyone odds that Kay's would out us in the final." [21] By the time he gets to *Mike and Psmith*, Wodehouse jests about the whole composition of the public-school novel. When Mike introduces himself to Psmith, Psmith asks, "Are you the Bully, the Pride of the School, or the Boy who is Led Astray and takes to Drink in Chapter Sixteen?" [22]

As Richard Usborne says, Wodehouse steers entirely clear of the worst clichés of his contemporaries and predecessors. If he is moral, he is not top-lofty. There is a strong code at work on the playing field, but there is nothing quixotic about the boys. When one of Wodehouse's cricket captains wins the toss, he does not, like Tom Brown, put the other team in first. He was young, all right, says Wodehouse, but not that young. And if Wodehouse is romantic, he is not morbid. With *The Old Curiosity Shop* and *Dombey and Son,* Dickens had made death scenes popular, and in the juvenile fiction of Dean Farrar, boys were always falling off cliffs, drowning, or just wasting away with disease. But in Wodehouse, though a boy may get mumps or sprain an ankle, he never goes to the infirmary with anything more serious.[23]

Because Wodehouse avoids the worst excesses and absurdities of contemporary fashion, it is easy to forget how long ago the school novels were written. It is not the essences of the books, but their accidents that give away their ages. For instance, the reader is suddenly reminded that *The Gold Bat* is an Edwardian book when Wodehouse catalogues the theatrical photographs on the walls of one boy's study: Sir Henry Irving in his costume for *The Bells*, Mrs. Patrick Campbell, Martin Harvey in *The Only Way,* and Seymour Hicks (not yet Sir Seymour). In the most recent edition of *Mike and Psmith* a revision intended to bring the book up to the present is actually a reminder of its place in the past. The name of a great runner of the day is changed to Bannister, who (the reader may reflect) was not even born in 1909. Unrevised, some of the slang in the books puts the stamp of an earlier time on occasional pages: "brekker" for breakfast; "got beans" for got reprimanded; "crocked" for injured; "mill" for fight or row.

V *The School Novels and the Later Work*

In some respects the world of the school novels is completely removed from that of all of the following novels. For one thing, it is a more serious world. Even if the boys have nothing more than a football match to be serious about, they are more solemn about it than adults are about graver matters. But they do well to be serious, for good and evil are real things, as they seldom are in the later novels, and there are real heroes and villains. When one boy says that he cannot imagine anybody being so low as to turn in the gold bat, thus ruining Trevor and the chances of the team, Trevor himself says that you cannot be sure: "He felt that this was but an outside chance. The forebearance of one's antagonist is but a poor thing to trust to at the best of times." [24]

Unlike the world of Bertie Wooster, in which the operations of cause and effect are suspended and a *deus ex machina* is always in readiness, the world of the school stories is one in which people must pay the consequences of their crimes and their errors. At Christmas time Mike's father tells him that he will have to leave Wrykyn if his next report is no better than the current one. The next report is not better, but worse, and Mike is forthwith transferred to Sedleigh. Though he is unhappy about his fate, he can only bow to it, for there is no Jeeves to whom he can appeal.

Insofar as time is not arrested in the school novels, they are more real than the later novels. Comic characters like Barmy Fotheringay-Phipps and Gussie Kink-Nottle are fixed forever at one age and confined once and for all in one system of responses. They learn nothing, and they forget nothing. The schoolboys, however, grow and change and they have, furthermore, an awareness of possibility and variety both in themselves and in others. Also their views of the older people on whom they necessarily depend are those of real boys. Adults can inspire a broad range of emotions: admiration, affection, indifference, disgust, contempt. The uncle or the aunt has not yet become the fat figure of fun or the poison-breathing dragon of the later books.

At the same time, the school stories contain some anticipations of the books to come. First, the Wodehouse style is already fairly well formed. The sense of phrase is so far developed that one may be brought up in surprise by a rare lapse into the clumsy syntax of third-rate fiction like the following: " 'I hope the dickens it's nothing to do with that bally report,' was his muttered exclamation." [25] Though the sentence structure is simpler than it will be later, some passages in a more complex style clearly indicate that Wodehouse is confining himself within the simplicities of school fiction. A strictly boys' book passage like the following is obviously deliberate: "Everything seemed black to him, a black, surging mist, and in its center a thin, white line, the tape. Could he reach it before Drake, or would he collapse before he reached it? There were only five more yards to go now, and still he led. Four, three. Two. Then something swept past him on the right, the white line quivered, snapped, and vanished, and he pitched blindly forward onto the turf at the track-side. Drake had won by a foot." [26]

The prose of the school novels is characterized by the quotation, paraphrase, and allusion that mark the later books. Wodehouse uses tags of Latin, "Solvitur ambulando"; the Bible, "Thieves break in and steal"; Shakespeare, a bewildered eye, "rolling in a fine frenzy from heaven to earth, and from earth to heaven"; Gilbert and Sullivan; Arthur Conan Doyle; and others. Moreover, he has begun to use a number of phrases which will be favorite ones through all the later writing: "the iron had entered his soul"; "it was but the work of a moment"; "turn your giant brain to this"; and so on. The first reference to Eugene Aram, who virtually amounts to an obsession with Bertie Wooster, occurs in *The Head of Kay's*. To be sure, Wodehouse is not as deft with quotation and allusion as he is in the books to follow. In *The Head of Kay's* he plunks down, in the middle of the page, a long extract from *H. M. S. Pinafore*, whereas in a later novel, he would weave it in. But even at the beginning he has acquired a control that enables him to juggle the stately Greek of Thucydides with the English nonsense of Lewis Carroll.

Some of the basic situations and standard characters of the later romantic and comic novels are first sketched out, with more somber colors, in the school novels. As Richard Usborne says, Mike's friend Wyatt and Mr. Wain introduce the figures of the orphan, the stepparent, and the authority to whom harassment of the young is either a primary duty or a passionate hobby. Wyatt has neither father nor mother, and his stepfather is also his housemaster. Because Mr. Wain is as dreadful in the one capacity as he is in the other, the relation between him and Wyatt is a kind of uneasy neutrality with intervals of frank hostility. A quarrel rather worse than the ordinary proves too much for such bonds as there are between the two, and Wyatt leaves Mr. Wain as the romantic hero Joe Vanringham will later leave his stepmother the Princess.

Though in the school stories the aunt figure has not moved into the center of the stage, she is at least waiting in the wings. In the second novel, more than one boy is getting letters from an aunt who appears to have nothing better to do than pester defenseless nephews. Wodehouse did not have to borrow Wilde's Aunt Augusta to create Aunt Agatha, as he has been charged with doing. From the start he had aunts on his mind, and Agatha is simply the most powerful in a succession of Wodehouse models.

Even the characteristics of the heroes of the later novels are beginning to evolve in the school books. The boy Charteris in the first school book is gradually transformed into the older boy Psmith of the last school book. Charteris' gift of gab and habit of quotation descend to Psmith and become more sophisticated. Then, in *Psmith in the City* (1910), Psmith nearly turns himself into the first of the mature heroes (in *Leave It to Psmith* [1923] he arrives at maturity) who have moved out of the school world and into the world of London restaurants, village inns, golf courses, drinks, and girls. While still in the school world, Psmith anticipates not only the brash and gabby heroes of the light romances, but also the bumbling non-heroes of the comedies. For to the foppery of words Psmith adds the more obvious foppery of dress and attitude. Like the romantic heroes, Psmith can acquit himself in any brawl that happens to come up (in *Mike at Wrykyn* he throws another boy out of a window, and in *Psmith in the City* he fights a London "proletarian"); but he much prefers languor to action. He dresses meticulously, and he affects an eye-

[64]

glass. Wodehouse has only to keep the fluency of Psmith (though making the quotations somewhat shaky and subject to confirmation by Jeeves) and to emphasize Psmith's languid, non-athletic side to go a long way toward the creation of Bertie Wooster.

CHAPTER 3

Experiments and Transitions

I Love and Ukridge

IN 1906, with three school novels to go, Wodehouse tried his hand at writing fiction for adults in a novel called *Love Among the Chickens*. The hero of this novel is in some respects rather like the heroes of the light romantic novels that Wodehouse was to write later, and in others like the heroes of the comic novels (for instance, he has an uncle who will give him an allowance as soon as he marries). He may also be a self-portrait of Wodehouse in his middle twenties. For Jeremy Garnet is a devotee of the cult of fitness, a swimmer, golfer, tennis player, and perhaps even performer of Swedish exercises. He is also a devotee of the cult of the pipe, which, by public school standards, is more manly than cigarettes. In process of establishing himself as a writer of light fiction, he is self-conscious about his profession, on the one hand proud to be a practicing "author," and on the other hand apologetic because he is not a profound one. The diffidence that he feels emerges in the form of a defensive anti-intellectualism that will be part of the point of view of all the novels to follow. ". . . I, Jeremy Garnet," he says, "harmless, well-meaning writer of minor novels. . . ." [1] In his period of greatest frustration, he professes to see a recompense to come in his writing: "Jerry Garnet, the man, might become a depressed, hopeless wreck, with the iron planted immovably in his soul; but Jeremy Garnet, the Author, should turn out such a novel of gloom that strong critics would weep, and the public jostle for copies. . . ." [2]

For the first time, readers of Wodehouse are introduced to a grown girl and a love affair. On a railway journey from London to Lyme Regis (changed to Combe Regis in later editions), Garnet meets Professor Derrick and his daughter Phyllis. The carriage in which they travel is the scene of some low comedy between a Gilbertian aunt and a bumptious nephew, but their goings-on are not enough to break the spell that Phyllis instantly casts on Garnet. Later, staying at the chicken farm of his friend Ukridge, he pursues a hen through a hedge and meets Phyllis again. Properly introduced, he begins to dance an extremely decorous attendance upon her. In what he imagines to be a rivalry for the love of Phyllis between himself and a young Naval officer, Garnet is guided and constrained by the public school code of honor. Though he has got in disgrace with Phyllis' father and would like to ask Lieutenant Tom Chase to intercede for him, he cannot in conscience do so. In a syntax as stiff as his rectitude, he explains why: "I felt that I must play the game. To request one's rival to give assistance in the struggle, to the end that he may be more readily cut out, can hardly be considered cricket." [3] Fortunately, Chase loves Phyllis' sister, not Phyllis, so Garnet's suit is eventually successful.

Garnet's love affair, modeled on the popular novels of the time, is a more sentimental business than any of the love affairs in the later books. Garnet moons under the drawing-room windows of Phyllis' house every night until he is chilled and soaked with dew. He talks about her to a dog named Bob and even to a star (unnamed). But since his love is such a sacred thing, he is reticent as well as extravagant. Of the crucial love scene he says, "Somehow we had stopped, as if by agreement, and were facing each other. There was a look in her eyes I had never seen there before. The twilight hung like a curtain between us and the world. We were alone together in a world of our own." [4] Into this world the reader is not admitted very far. Garnet declares his love in the last line of the chapter, and Phyllis accepts him between chapters. The following chapter begins with a discussion of the problem of getting the consent of Professor Derrick.

In spite of its absurd sentimentality, the book has a good deal of charm even today, and Garnet is not altogether a sentimental fool. Indeed, he sometimes speaks a bitter wisdom that might have come from the *Maxims* of La Rochefoucauld: "One can pardon any injury to oneself, unless it hurts one's vanity"; and ". . . everyone instinctively dislikes being under an obligation which they can never wholly repay." [5] He does not, however, speak often in this spirit, which is alien to his essential nature and to the whole atmosphere of the novel. For the world of *Love*

Among the Chickens is, if anything, more naïve and innocent than the world of the school novels. In the first place, it is the Edwardian world. Wodehouse published the book in 1906, and though he changed the price of eggs in the 1921 edition, he did not change much else. In *Love Among the Chickens*, people still take trouble to maintain good croquet lawns, and they still go to Mudie's for their books. Girls carry sketch books, and young couples sing duets after dinner. Manners are so formal that Jeremy calls Phyllis Miss Derrick and she calls him Mr. Garnet after they have known each other for a whole summer, and it takes their engagement to bring them to first names.

Aside from an opening section in London and the chapter on the train, the story takes place in an idyllic Devonshire of blue skies, lovely sunsets, and sheep bells tinkling in the quiet dusk. Everybody is on vacation. Though Garnet is working on a novel, he is at Lyme Regis on a kind of holiday. Tom Chase is on leave from the British Navy, and World War I is eight years away. Phyllis is spending her usual summer with her father, a musical-comedy academic whose discipline remains a mystery and whose duties apparently require him to spend very little time at his university. To the charm of innocence and youth, Wodehouse adds the buoyancy of irresponsibility.

Wodehouse was to become in later books a plot-maker of remarkable ingenuity, but all of the vital events in the romance between Jeremy and Phyllis are completely foreseeable. If Garnet cannot, the reader can guess that Tom Chase is no rival of Garnet's. As soon as the golf match between Garnet and the Professor is arranged, the reader surmises that Garnet will allow the Professor to win, in exchange for his consent to marry Phyllis. Garnet does not get the idea of driving such a bargain until he is driving off the eighteenth tee. Moreover, Wodehouse uses in a romantic context such devices of plot as he will later use only in a comic one. In an earlier attempt to ingratiate himself with the Professor, Garnet bribes a boatman to tip Professor Derrick into the sea, and then swims out to save him and become a hero. This moronic stratagem will become a favorite one in the circle of Bertie Wooster. Garnet knows that it is a cliché of magazine romances, and he has in fact used it himself in half a dozen stories.

At this stage, however, Wodehouse allows the clichés at least a marginal validity.

As the title indicates, there is comedy in the novel as well as romance, and if comedy is not the dominant note, it is the closing one. The chapter in which Garnet tells Phyllis that he loves her is followed by three chapters largely concerned with the golf match, and these are followed by three that bring the business of the chicken farm to a conclusion. Some of the comedy is no better and no worse than the situation comedy of television. Important guests are invited to a dinner that goes from one disaster to another. Forbidden topics of conversation are introduced. A comic dog and a comic cat contribute something to the imbroglios (but much less to the comedy than the cat Augustine and Stiffy Byng's terrier Bartholomew do in subsequent books).

A comedy more characteristic of Wodehouse appears in the person and the enterprises of Stanley Featherstonehaugh Ukridge, Garnet's erratic friend. A long letter from William Townend about the sorry attempts of a friend of his to get rich quickly by raising chickens, provided Wodehouse with the beginnings of the main comic plot of the novel and the character of Ukridge. Wodehouse also used his own memories of a schoolmate addicted to borrowing clothes, and Richard Usborne shrewdly guesses that Doyle's James Cullingworth served as a third model.[6] At all events, Ukridge is the first of Wodehouse's non-heroes. He is a false Achates, rushing in and out of others' lives, invariably bringing trouble with him. Cadging (drinks, money, or anything else that he needs at the moment) is so deeply ingrained in him that it amounts to a tropism. But he would not be so bad if he merely wanted to pick people's pockets. He also wants to run their careers, imagining, perhaps, that by involving them in his cretinish schemes he is repaying them for whatever he has mooched from them. Thus he drags Garnet down to the chicken farm. (A note from a mutual friend, warning Garnet that Ukridge was in London, arrives too late for Garnet to flee.) His efforts to help Garnet in his love affair with Phyllis consist of infuriating Professor Derrick by talking of the Irish question and Edward Carson (subjects of which Ukridge is completely ignorant) and nearly drowning the Professor by swimming after him to badger him.

One need not be a friend of Ukridge to suffer for Ukridge's sins, for he is a menace not only to a small circle of acquaintances, but also to the whole of respectable society. The merchants who sell him the chickens and the tradesmen at Lyme Regis who provide him with food, pictures, a gramophone, a piano, and so on, are only a few in a long series of victims. Since they ultimately get their money, they are at least more fortunate than a tailor with whom Ukridge deals earlier in his career. Ukridge buys two suits from the tailor on the installment plan, paying a small sum in advance. He pawns one of the suits to pay the first few installments, and then he disappears. Following his usual custom, he has given a false name "as an ordinary business precaution." As for the address, the tailor eventually finds that it is a deserted house, empty except for the series of bills that he has mailed there.

Ukridge is Wodehouse's first essay in the picaresque. Besides setting up as a chicken farmer, he has taught in prep schools and sailed on tramp steamers. (At one point a friend tells Garnet that the last he heard of Ukridge, was that the lout had gone to Buenos Aires on a cattle ship, his luggage consisting of a borrowed pipe.) For the most part, he lives by his wits, such as they are, by a succession of diverse theories, each as dogmatically held as the one that preceded it, and by his spirit, which is indomitable. No other man has been so fertile in schemes for making money, and no other man has such a consistent record of failure. But from the ruins of each scheme Ukridge looks brightly out to the next one, plans his simple-minded strategy, and (if possible) ropes in a friend.

Ukridge is no more of a nitwit than many another character in Wodehouse, but he is a good deal more of a scoundrel. Garnet says that the proceedings on the chicken farm would be amusing if it were not for the fact that Ukridge's wife Millie has to be distressed by them. Millie's Aunt Elizabeth hates Ukridge (he returns her hate and names the most troublesome hen on the farm after her.) For once, an aunt in Wodehouse appears to be in the right, and a nephew in the wrong. Wodehouse himself evidently regards the Ukridge of *Love Among the Chickens* as too much of a good thing, at least too much to be inflicted on Millie. In the later stores about Ukridge, Wodehouse goes backward in time to bachelor days, so that Millie is excluded from the list of casualties.

But Wodehouse early recognized Ukridge's major comic value. In the first edition of *Love Among the Chickens*, Ukridge's affairs at the chicken farm are settled, and then there is an epilogue, a little play that recounts the wedding of Jeremy and Phyllis. In the 1921 revision, however, there is no epilogue, and Ukridge has the last word. First he makes an eloquent speech denouncing and dismissing his creditors. When they have gone, he turns to Garnet and begins to tell him of his newest brainstorm: a duck farm on which the ducks have no access to bodies of water. His theory is that ducks gain weight slowly because they swim around all the time. It follows, then, that ducks without ponds will fatten with great rapidity. In the final lines of the novel, Ukridge is estimating the profits to be got from such an enterprise, so much the first year, so much the second, and so on.

With the successful conclusion of their romance, Jeremy Garnet and Phyllis Derrick pass out of the Wodehouse world, but Ukridge remains to become one of the most important comic characters in it. Between 1924 and 1950 Wodehouse published seventeen stories about him. Ukridge was good for a succession of stories, since, never learning anything from an experience, he could always go on to another of a similar sort. The costumes that Wodehouse ran up for him in the early years were so successful that they have remained unchanged. Perhaps the most conspicuous article of Ukridge's dress is his dirty mackintosh, which he wears in all weathers, sometimes over dirty flannels, sometimes over pyjamas. His tennis shoes are absolutely filthy, and falling off his feet. A literal as well as a figurative myope, he wears a pince-nez, but the spring that should keep the spectacles on by gripping the bridge of his nose is defective. He therefore fastens them to his ears with ginger-beer wire (though ginger-beer had long ago ceased to be sold in stone bottles which have wire to keep in the corks).

In *Love Among the Chickens*, Wodehouse also established Ukridge's speech, the basis of which is standard Wodehouse. In common with Garnet, for instance, Ukridge paraphrases Tennyson. (From the basement of the house in Lyme Regis, Garnet hears the "murmur of innumerable fowls." [7] Ukridge complains that the tradesmen of the area are "as deficient in Simple Faith as they are in Norman blood." [8]) Ukridge also speaks in the vigorously incongruous idiom of other Wodehouse characters. When one of the chicken merchants asks him if he would like some Minorcas, Ukridge, to whom a chicken is a chicken, replies impatiently: "Very well, unleash the Minorcas." [9] But Wodehouse also gives Ukridge sole title to certain expressions like "old horse," which he applies to old friends, strangers in the street, and (once) to a bishop, and "upon my Sam," earlier a favorite of the boys in Kipling's *Stalky and Co.*

II Enter Psmith

In 1909 Wodehouse published *Mike*, the last, longest, and best of the school novels. The first half of *Mike*, later published as *Mike at Wrykyn*, has already been discussed. The second half, later published as *Enter Psmith* and as *Mike and Psmith*, is in many respects much like all of the other school fiction, but is in others significantly different. Sports are still a major occupation of the boys, and cricket games constitute the crucial spots halfway through and at the close of the action. Though Mike's resentment at being transferred from Wrykyn to Sedleigh keeps him out of all important school matches until the very last, he plays regularly for the village team. In common with most of the other boys, Mike cannot imagine a better life than that of his brother Joe, an estate agent to a sporting baronet who considers that Joe's chief duty is playing cricket for his county. (Mike, indeed, is later sent to Cambridge by Psmith's father, is then hired as his agent, and presumably plays cricket on every possible occasion.) The other occupations also remain much the same. There are mild rags, pranks, and breakings-out. Mike is suspected not only of ringing the school fire-alarm bell (correctly), but also of painting the school dog (incorrectly, since no good schoolboy would do such a thing, though a bad old boy would and did). There is trouble with a tyrannical housemaster who is properly frustrated and ultimately defeated.

Mike and Psmith differs from the other school novels because Psmith enters the school and becomes Mike's friend. The friendship of Mike and Psmith is an attraction of opposites and a study in contrasts, a bond between the boy who is the most sophisticated in the school novels and the boy who is perhaps the least. Mike is the schoolboy ideal of the athlete, a spectacular figure on the cricket field, already in some ways a greater delight to watch than his older brothers. Off the field, however, he is a pretty dim figure, if not the type of the dumb athlete, at least a shy and diffident one, as awkward in social life as he is agile in sports. He does not know what to say to people of a different age and class from himself unless they are cricketers. Not that he is any more snobbish than the next boy. He intuitively understands the people whom he likes, and he can be made miserable by the sight of anybody's suffering. But he is simply tongue-tied. (He continues to be inarticulate in the following book, *Psmith in the City*, even with his great friend Psmith. When, at the end of the book, Psmith has arranged Mike's future for him, Mike can get no nearer to expressing his gratitude than saying, "I say, Psmith." [10]) Mike is still mentally and emotionally young enough to be perfectly comfortable in a school, perfectly contented with its licit and its forbidden fruits. For example, he thinks that it is a great adventure to sneak into the housemaster's dining room in the middle of the night, steal the biscuits, and turn on the gramophone.

Psmith, on the contrary, has already gone beyond the school world and his schoolboy self when he arrives at Sedleigh. He talks of his youth and even of his riper years as if they were long past. Instead of shouting and rushing about like his fellows, he speaks in a tired voice (like Aldous Huxley's Mrs. Viveash) and moves languidly. He would not get up in the middle of the night to steal biscuits or break out, nor would he get up early to practice fielding, since both sorts of enterprise would interfere with his sleep. He likes to breakfast as late as possible and, no doubt, would prefer to breakfast in bed as Bertie Wooster does. An eccentric, Psmith likes all kinds of people, takes an interest in their problems, and (unlike the clumsy Ukridge) helps them instead of making matters worse. His way of helping them, however, is rather Flammonde-like, and he patronizes everybody from the school sergeant to the headmaster. Though he says that he is a Socialist, and calls everyone "Comrade," the term is as often condescending or insulting as it is cordial. Finally, Psmith is one of Wodehouse's nonstop talkers; were it not for his vein of irony, one might mistake Psmith's fluency for logomania. Sometimes his constant chitchat has a strategic purpose, for Psmith, though a decent enough cricket player and a tough enough fighter when obliged to brawl, prefers to dominate groups and to get his way with words. But if there is no purpose, the talk still flows, and if Psmith has nothing to talk about, he will make up something.

With *Mike and Psmith*, Wodehouse is done with the public school novel. There will be no more schoolboy heroes and no more public school backgrounds, except for purposes of farce (reunions of old boys, for example, in which bishops climb up and down the waterspouts of the dormitories). But in the next novel, *Psmith in the City*, the ties to the school are still strong. There are no accounts of school matches, but at the end of the novel Mike plays in a county match when one of his brother Joe's teammates falls ill. At the start of the book, Mike's father has lost most of his money, and Mike is going to work in a London bank instead of going to a university. He takes a room in Dulwich, not only because he believes that it will be cheaper than one in London, but also because there is a school in Dulwich, and a school means cricket. The sight of the cricket field, however, only depresses him. "Up to now the excitement of a strange adventure had borne him up; but the cricket-field and the pavilion reminded him so sharply of Wrykyn. They brought home to him with a cutting distinctness the absolute finality of the break with the old order of things. Summers would come and go, matches would be played on this ground with all the glory of big scores and keen finishes; but he was done. . . . Top of the Wrykyn averages two years. But didn't do anything after he left. Went into the City or something." [11]

Mike, however, gets a warm welcome from the other clerks in the bank when they learn that he is one of the cricket-playing Jacksons (for the bank, like corporations in our own time, has teams). Another good thing about the bank (Mike does not find very many up to the day he leaves) is that there is a kind of spirit in it that somewhat resembles a school spirit. Everyone is working for one purpose, is doing, in a sense, one kind of work. Yet it is impossible for Mike to love the bank as he loved his school: "There is a cold impersonality about a bank. A school is a living thing." [12] When, at the close of the novel, Mike and Psmith walk out of the bank during working hours, Mike to play cricket at Lord's and Psmith to watch him, their defiance of the bank manager is like a victory over a bad schoolmaster.

Psmith, however, dominates the novel even more than he does the earlier one. As a consequence, many of the ties with school are cut, and new ones are established in their stead. Like Mike, Psmith works in the bank, but not out of any financial need. In his patronizing way, he once commented upon the bridge-playing of the bank manager, Mr. Bickersdyke, when Bickersdyke was staying with the Psmith family in Shropshire. To get revenge, Bickersdyke suggested that it would do Psmith a world of good to have a job in the City. Psmith's father, a man of enthusiasms as sudden and transient as they are passionate, agreed. Psmith, however, does not live like an ordinary bank clerk. He is ensconced in a very comfortable bachelor flat, and from this headquarters he ranges the London clubs (his father takes out memberships for him in a dozen, from the Senior Conservative to the Drones), the theaters, and the restaurants. Thus begin the countless suppers at the Savoy that the later heroes of Wodehouse, romantic and comic alike, will consume. At this point, there are no girls, but there are cigars and wine in plenty. Psmith, as Richard Usborne says, takes us from the cricket field to Piccadilly.[13]

The note of snobbery is stronger in *Psmith in the City* than it is in the school stories, perhaps because there are more sounding boards for it. In the school stories, the lower classes are almost by definition low comedians, court fools without wit. The fact that they speak a language inferior to that of the schoolboys is in itself enough to prevent their affairs, including their love affairs, from being taken seriously. Thus it is when Psmith encounters the parlor-maid and the postman at his housemaster's door: "Psmith stood by politely till the postman, who had just been told it was like his impudence, caught sight of him, and, having handed over the letters in an ultra-formal and professional manner, passed away." [14]

In *Psmith in the City*, the idioms and accents of tram conductors and policemen are more barbarous than those of postmen and parlor-maids; they are also exploited more extensively and treated with greater irony: "The conductor deposed that he had bin on the point of pushing on, seeing as how he'd hung abart long enough, when he see'd them two gents, the long 'un with the heye-glass (Psmith bowed) and t'other 'un a-legging of it dahn the road towards him. . . ."; "Lucidly and excellently put," says Psmith.[15]

For the first time in the novels, the lower classes appear in really large crowds, on Clapham Common, for instance, listening to a speaker who himself scatters aitches "as a fountain its sprays in a strong wind."[16] The electorate in Kenningford, S. E., Wodehouse says, contains a group of Liberals and a group of Unionists, but it also contains a group (presumably the largest of the lot) that regards elections simply as an opportunity for raising hell. If the people in this group vote at all, they vote irresponsibly, casting their ballots for the man who tells the best stories about his opponent. Psmith uses the expression "the many-headed" to describe the crowd on Clapham Common, and both of the boys use the school term "bargee." This term now connotes not only a member of the lower orders, but also a stupid lout, a loafer, a vulgarian in a cloth cap, a roughneck who likes to start riots in public places.

There is, in short, a new notion of the lower classes, that of the mob, together with a contempt for the mob, and also a certain fear of it. Mike and Psmith are forced to flee from a mob to the tram of the conductor who deposed above. Fighting at any reasonable odds, however, the public school boys are still superior, for the boxing style of the lower classes is unscientific and inelegant. That of the fellow whom Psmith fights is, Wodehouse says, a combination of windmill and turtle.

The sense of belonging to the public school world is also stronger in the city than in the school itself. Since the school walls no longer separate the boys from the rest of the world, perhaps it is necessary to erect walls of another sort. In any case, Mike is pleased to find that most of the men in the bank (with the exception of a few Scotsmen) are old public school men. In the first week alone, he discovers two Old Wrykynians: ". . . it was pleasing to have them about, and to feel that they had been educated at the right place."[17] But the bank manager is evidently not a public school man. Certainly Mr. Bickersdyke's cricket is no better than his bridge, and Psmith refers to him as a "bargee."

For a self-made man to order an Old Wrykynian like Mike and

an Old Etonian like Psmith about the bank is intolerable, as bad as it would be for the "usher" type of schoolmaster to nag them in their studies. Psmith, therefore, persecutes Bickersdyke without mercy, patronizing him in the bank, trailing after him at his club, humiliating him at a public meeting when he is standing for Parliament. Bickersdyke plans to get revenge by firing Psmith in front of half of the bank personnel, but Psmith forestalls the plan by resigning. Bickersdyke would murder Psmith with pleasure, but Psmith, with his usual irony, professes regret and surprise when, at the end of the novel, he recalls his relationship with the banker: ". . . it seemed to me sometimes, during our festive evenings together at the club, that all was not well. From little, almost imperceptible signs I have suspected now and then that he would just as soon have been without my company." [18]

III *Psmith in America*

In the next Psmith novel, *Psmith Journalist* (1915),[19] Mike and Psmith have just finished their first year at Cambridge. Mike has scored a century against Oxford, and Psmith has condescended to play a bit of nonchalant cricket. Though Psmith is kind enough to regard Cambridge as a pleasant place, he also considers that it might conceivably be rather more lively. When Mike leaves for a tour of what Wodehouse calls "the cricket-playing section of the United States," [20] Psmith accompanies him in the hope that New York will provide "a tolerably spacious rag." [21] One would expect *Psmith Journalist* to be a much better book than *Psmith in the City*, which is a good one. Between the two books, Wodehouse published five others, including the first volume in the Blandings Castle cycle. If the reader did not know that still better books followed, he might suppose that when Wodehouse came to write *Psmith Journalist*, he was already at the top of his form. The intervening books apart, there is an extremely good reason why *Psmith Journalist* ought to be a better book than its predecessor. Mike soon disappears on his cricket tour and returns for only two or three brief intervals, so that the novel is almost wholly Psmith's.

Nonetheless, *Psmith Journalist* is not superior to *Psmith in the City*, but much inferior. Though Psmith is older by a year and Wodehouse is older by five, though the other characters are adults, the entire novel is more juvenile than any of the school novels. Wodehouse now has a greater knowledge of the world, but the book is more provincial than the ones that went before. He tries to deal with real things, but the result is less realistic than any of his other work. No doubt the unfamiliar background of Broadway and gangsters made the earlier editions of the novel successful. But one cannot imagine American boys reading the book today, and one can scarcely understand how it has been reprinted again and again in England, most recently in 1950.

After five or six years in the United States, the Wodehouse of *Psmith Journalist* sees the country as an Englishman who had only read of it might see it. He points out that the apartment of the newspaperman Billy Windsor contains a typewriter (since no one in New York ever uses a pen), that the settee becomes a bed by night, that on the walls are hides, knives, and other mementos of Billy's prairie days, including the head of a young bear over the door. Then he says that a small New York apartment is much like a public school study. Likewise, he talks as if nurseries were as common in American houses as in English ones, and as if there were a kind of journalist whose title is "sub-editor." He does not even come near the actual language of his characters. For instance, prize fighters say "chaps," and "I shouldn't be able to," but at other times they are excessively illiterate. So are office boys and gangsters, whose "dat's," "der's," and "dis's" are tedious to read, and whose strongest oaths ("by Gum!") make ordinary euphemisms sound like salty talk.

At this period, Wodehouse regards America in terms of a somewhat sappy adventure and romance. Though Billy Windsor lives in New York City and works as the managing editor of a wretched magazine called *Cozy Moments* (in British fashion, Wodehouse calls it a paper), he was born on a Wyoming ranch. At the time of the novel's action, he is only twenty-five, but he has already worked on a Wyoming newspaper (where it is the custom of editors to keep guns on their desks) and on a paper in the feud country of Kentucky. In this school of journalism, he has lost one ear lobe and acquired a long scar across his left shoulder. He would look more natural, says Wodehouse, riding a broncho or cooking his dinner over a campfire than sitting in an editor's chair.

Wodehouse also sees the United States in terms of a sentimental moral contrast between the frontier and the city. Wyoming has given Billy Windsor muscles as tough as steel, but a heart as soft as a grape. Before the story proper even opens, he has rescued Pugsy Maloney, the office boy, from a beating and perhaps death in the street. Pugsy, in turn, rescues a lost cat from its tormentors. To restore the cat's tissues, as Psmith would say, Billy gives Pugsy a dollar to buy a bottle of milk and tells him to keep the change (milk costs five cents). As far as Billy is concerned, the whole East is corrupt, and one must go to Wyoming to get a square deal, presumably with gun and knife. Yet he is as fascinated by New York as he is repelled by it, and his ambition is to get a job on one of the big dailies.

Like Billy, Wodehouse himself is both repelled and attracted by New York. He is shocked by corrupt politicians and crooked elections, horrified by violence so incredible that it requires a preface for the benefit of British readers. "The conditions of life in New York are so different from those in London that a story of this kind calls for a little explanation. . . . Not all [of the inhabitants of New York] eke out a precarious livelihood by murdering one another, but there is a definite section of the population which murders—not casually, on the spur of the moment, but on definitely commercial lines at so many dollars a murder. The 'gangs' of New York exist in fact. I have not invented them." [22]

But violence and evil are at the same time attractive. Broadway, says Wodehouse, is "the Great White Way, the longest, straightest, brightest, wickedest street in the world." [23] Early in the novel Wodehouse deplores the great play that newspapers make over murder, gangsters, and so on, but when Psmith takes over *Cozy Moments*, he turns it into a tabloid of the most sensational sort. If Wodehouse pictures a New York of monstrous gangs, he also pictures one of brutal police. To prod people with their nightsticks is virtually a compulsion of the law officers in *Psmith Journalist*. In the middle of the night they drag innocent citizens to the police station in their pyjamas, and anyone who does not snap to it is stimulated by a short jab.

Wodehouse's conception of the gang leader is remarkably naïve. Bat Jarvis is the head of one of the four biggest gangs in New York, but he has all the earmarks of a small-time hoodlum. As a blind for his criminal activities, he keeps a pet shop. Even as a petty criminal, Bat is no more believable than the hoodlums in Damon Runyon. A sentimental thug and particularly fond of cats, he is so grateful to Billy Windsor for returning his lost cat to him that he vows to do anything to help if Windsor should ever be in trouble. When Windsor and Psmith run up against another gang, Bat is as good as his word. No one since Dick Whittington has ever got so much profit from a cat. An older and more sophisticated Wodehouse was to transform Bat Jarvis into such intentionally comic figures as Soup Slattery, the amiable safe-cracker.

Evidently, Wodehouse was even more appalled by New York slums than he was by New York gangs. "The New York slum . . . is unique. The height of the houses and the narrowness of the streets seem to condense its unpleasantness. All the smells and noises . . . are penned up in a sort of canyon, and gain in vehemence. . . . On the lower floors one could see into dark, bare rooms. These were the star apartments . . . for they opened on to the street and so got a little light and air. The imagination jibbed at the thought of the back rooms." [24] Indeed, Wodehouse gets sufficiently interested in the slum question to work up some of the material on it, the dodges of slum landlords, the way they hide behind their agents and their stooges, and so on. He even turns Psmith from a *flâneur* into a crusader. Having seen the dreadful slums, Psmith is at last deeply moved by something: "Here he had touched the realities. There was something worth fighting for. His lot had been cast in pleasant places, and the sight of actual raw misery had come home to him with an added force from that circumstance." [25]

The sympathy for the dwellers in the slums and the indignation against those who exploit them are admirable, but Wodehouse's remedy for the slums is about as adequate as a Band-Aid on a cancer. Psmith writes a series of articles denouncing the slum landlord, and the landlord's strong men threaten and then try to murder Psmith and Windsor. At this point, Bat Jarvis calls in his gang to support the Psmith-Windsor cause. Unable to intimidate Psmith, the landlord surrenders to Psmith's terms. And what are they? To write a check sufficient to cover the costs of repairs to the buildings that he owns. Having brought the villain to his knees, Psmith changes *Cozy Moments* back to its original character (Windsor has got his job on a big newspaper) and sails for England to resume his studies at Cambridge.

Psmith Journalist was an ill-advised project because Wodehouse had no talent for realism and because he was not well acquainted with the kind of people he was writing about. Later, he was to do his best work by writing quite unrealistically about the kind of people he knew better. The saving grace of *Psmith Journalist* is Psmith, whose character it would take more than an Atlantic crossing and a few encounters with gangsters to change. Psmith comes to New York because he is looking for excitement, and the city, especially as Wodehouse sees it, is not, of course, without excitement. But Psmith makes sure that he will have some by arranging for some. It is through his connection with Billy Windsor and *Cozy Moments* that he has his adventures with the underworld.

The proprietor of *Cozy Moments* founded it as an antidote to yellow journalism. Aside from yellow journalism, what a sufficient antidote to *Cozy Moments* would be, it would be difficult to say. Edited by J. Felkin Wilberfloss, it includes, among other atrocities, "Moments in the Nursery," conducted by Luella Granville Waterman; "Moments Among the Masters," conducted by Wilberfloss himself and plagiarized outright from the great literature of the past, and "Moments with Budding Girlhood," conducted by Julia Burdett Parslow. When Psmith attaches himself to *Cozy Moments* as unpaid editor, he revamps the magazine in accord with the plan that he outlines to Billy Windsor: ". . . my idea is that *Cozy Moments* should become red-hot stuff. I could wish its tone to be such that the public will wonder why we do not print it on asbestos. We must chronicle all the live events of the day, murders, fires, and the like in a manner which will make our readers' spines thrill. Above all, we must be a search-light showing up the dark spots in the souls of those who would endeavor in any way to do THE PEOPLE in the eye." [26]

Psmith's feat of changing *Cozy Moments* into a paper that concentrates on sports, sensational news, and crusades and then changing it back to its original soppiness is probably the working out of a fantasy that the young Wodehouse had about some of the dreadful magazines for which he supplied copy. In later novels he frequently gives his heroes jobs on magazines that are, as he would say, unfit for human consumption. Even Bertie Wooster does a piece for his Aunt Dahlia's paper, *Milady's Boudoir*. After *Psmith Journalist,* however, Wodehouse is content to leave such rotten publications as they are, probably considering that it serves them jolly well right.

IV *Mike and Psmith as Antecedents*

The Mike and Psmith stories are extremely important in the career of Wodehouse, not only because they provide a bridge whereby the action is brought out of the school world and into the wider world of London and the counties, and New York as well, but also because they provide the qualities of character that go to make up the heroes of the novels that follow. The heroes of the light romantic novels are a composite of Mike and Psmith, a synthesis of the shy, tongue-tied athlete and the bold, articulate adventurer. Like Mike, these young fellows are endowed with extraordinary physical prowess. If they no longer play cricket or football, still they are capable of standing up to a whole street of villagers or London proletarians, disarming gunmen, climbing up walls and in and out of windows, swinging from one beam to another, and so on. It was appropriate that in the dramatization of *A Gentleman of Leisure,* a novel published in 1910, Douglas Fairbanks played the hero, Jimmy Pitt. The virility of Wodehouse's romantic heroes is indicated by their names, which are always manly and more often than not monosyllabic (Joe, Sam, George). Wodehouse would no longer even dream of giving a hero a name like Jeremy Garnet.

Like Psmith, the heroes of the romantic novels are impudent, resourceful, talented in intrigue, ruthless, and almost incapable of being ruffled. They stop at no stratagem to win the girls they love; they lightly patronize their employers (when they have any); and they generally go through the world (as one of them says of himself, quoting a popular song) with their hats on the sides of their heads. Like both Mike and Psmith, they are bound, in spite of their sometimes unconscionable behavior, to a few moral commandments that derive from the public school code. For instance, one does not let a friend down, and one does not sneak. If one may cheerfully lie to a girl to win her, one cannot

even consider breaking the engagement if one later discovers
that he does not love her.

More important, certain qualities in Psmith help to make up
the characters of the non-heroes of the comic novels, like Freddie
Threepwood and Bertie Wooster. For one thing, these fellows inherit Psmith's preference for London over the country. Freddie
devotes the greatest part of his energies to schemes to foil his father and get up to the Metropolis. Bertie has a flat in Berkley
Square, and in his perambulations through the city confines himself to the areas where the theaters, clubs, and fashionable restaurants are found. When he leaves the city to stay at a country
house, he always returns to London with relief, and probably
with one or two new wounds. For, although the sun may shine
upon Bertie when he sets out from London in his two-seater, the
journey is a perilous one; the country combines great dullness
with danger. The non-heroes also inherit Psmith's languidness.
They like to sink into soft chairs, stretch out their legs, and smoke,
thinking of nothing in particular by the hour. Even in repose,
they need frequent draughts of whisky, tea, or other refreshment
to sustain them. When they walk, they "toddle" or "totter."

Another legacy from Psmith is their concern for dress, but
whereas Psmith is blessed with fastidiousness, Bertie is cursed
with bad taste. Psmith says that he quit playing cricket once and
for all because, in a village match, he was caught at point by a
man wearing braces and has never got over the shock to his system. Bertie's wardrobe is enormous, but were it not for his valet,
Jeeves, it is doubtful if any one piece of apparel would match any
other, and some articles are absolutely execrable in themselves.

The snobbery of Psmith is somewhat modified in Bertie and his
peers. Though they use the same term for the lower classes that
Psmith does, "the many-headed," the contempt seems to have
gone out of it. When Bertie addresses working people with such
expressions as "my jolly old barmaid," he is not condescending
like Psmith, but speaking quite amiably in the idiom of the silly-
ass Englishmen. Still, Bertie does not particularly like or admire
people in the classes below his own, and he does not even have
Psmith's rather anthropological interest in them as representa-
tives of inferior cultures. The egotism of Psmith, which is less an ac-

tual preoccupation with the self than it is a conscious parody, a sustained stunt, becomes in Bertie a true absorption in a childish notion of himself which he has derived from the clichés of melodrama. Having arrived at Clapham Common in a cab, but been forced to flee from it in a tram, Psmith says to Mike, "Do you realize the thing that has happened? I am riding in a tram. I, Psmith, have paid a penny for a ticket . . . If this should get about the clubs. I tell you . . . no such crisis has ever occurred before in the course of my career." [27] Bertie likes to tell the reader that those who know the man Wooster well are aware of this or that quality, that on such and such an occasion he was a thing of fire and chilled steel, that he meant a sharp remark to sting, and so forth.

In yet another way, Psmith is of great importance to the later novels. Speech is vital to Wodehouse's fiction; and Richard Usborne points out that by isolating the elements of Psmith's incessant talk, Wodehouse obtains three different conversational styles for other characters.[28] In part, Psmith's speech is formal, literary, even pompous. It is larded with quotations and allusions, seasoned with archaic phrases and bits of pedantry. Whatever he may be talking about, Psmith prefers circumlocution to conciseness and elegant variation to simple Anglo-Saxon.

But the speech of Psmith is also a travesty of all this. He pushes the poetry around, mixes slang with classy diction, and indulges in conscious malapropisms. While still a schoolboy, he has his style fairly well developed. As Mike and Adair are about to fight in Psmith's study, Psmith says: "My dear young friends, if you *will* let your angry passions rise, against the direct advice of Doctor Watts, I suppose you must. But when you propose to claw each other . . . in the midst of a hundred fragile and priceless ornaments, I lodge a protest. . . . I don't want all the study furniture smashed. I know a bank where the wild thyme grows, only a few yards down the road, where you can scrap all night if you want to. How would it be to move on there? Any objections? None. Then shift ho! And let's get it over with." [29]

The first type of speech derived from Psmith's is that of Wodehouse's clever people, the young heroes of the light romantic novels (whether British or American, they speak the same language) and such perennial undergraduates as Uncle Fred and Lancelot

Threepwood. Their idiom is Psmith's transformed into a more sophisticated one. They are no less fluent than he, and they have a faster tempo. They also patronize right and left, not with Psmith's sometimes lymphatic stateliness, but with a cool and impudent wit. Like Psmith, they quote, but whereas Psmith's intonation is an equivalent of quotation marks, they—more subtle—have mastered the art of throwing away quoted lines.

The second type of speech drawn from Psmith's is that of Wodehouse's morons. A kind of shaky translation from Psmith, it is the tongue of Bingo Little and Freddie Threepwood; it is, indeed, the patois of the Drones Club, and it is brought to perfection by the noblest Drone of them all, Bertie Wooster. Bertie loves words as much as any of the clever heroes, and he shoots words out as rapidly as they, but they are professsionals, and he is a bemused amateur. Though he can quote with the best of them, his notions as to the sources of his quotations are, more often than not, foggy. "Not one of my things," he will say by way of acknowledgment, "one of Jeeves'," and the reader will recognize that Jeeves has himself quoted from Shakespeare. If Bertie knows more words than any other character in Wodehouse (and he probably does), he does not always know their meanings. Recognizing his own unreliability, he often interpolates, "If that is the word I want." As for the deliberate incongruity in Psmith's speech, in Bertie's it becomes a sheer and inspired inability to discriminate, and Bertie is as likely to say, "And that right speedily," in any spot of conversation as he is to say, "And look slippy about it."

The third type of speech is that of Jeeves. Whether Jeeves is bringing Bertie breakfast or a hangover remedy, laying out his clothes or outlining a scheme for blackmail, his speech stems from the formal strain in Psmith's. It is superbly suited to his wisdom (it is right that an oracle should have a certain linguistic dignity) and it serves to make him thoroughly respectful and, at the same time, completely unapproachable.

A fourth style deriving from Psmith's is Wodehouse's own. The voice of Psmith is first heard in the last of the school novels and next in *Psmith in the City*. From then on, with negligible exceptions, Wodehouse will never write in the lucid but straightforward narrative style of the school stories. Instead, the style of the author, without losing its clarity, will take on the quotation and allusion, the paraphrase and parody, the incongruous mixture of vocabularies with which some of the earlier schoolboys experimented and which Psmith exploited to create his own idiom. But Wodehouse will purge and refine the schoolboy cleverness, the loquacity and affectation of Psmith into a style that is light, lucid, concise, witty, allusive—one of the most skillful styles and one of the best suited to its purpose in twentieth-century British fiction.

CHAPTER 4

The Light Romances

I Derivations

BY 1910 Wodehouse was done with school fiction. In the dozens upon dozens of volumes that followed the school novels, he devoted himself to light novels of love and adventure, to farce, and to mixtures of the two modes. The straight love stories are not numerous, and Wodehouse soon increased the proportion of comedy in the mixed novels. Since World War II he has written mostly farce comedy. The light romances of the previous thirty years stem from Wodehouse's own earlier work and from several literary traditions. They are nurtured by a side of Wodehouse's nature that has always contended with his comic spirit. Their typical characters and settings are derived, first, from his experiences as a child and young man in England; second, from his later experiences as a very successful writer of novels, plays, and musical comedies, living part of the time in England and on the Continent, and part of the time in the United States. The weaknesses of the light romances are sentimentality and melodrama. Their strength is Wodehouse's counter inclination to treat love humorously and to turn melodrama into comedy.

Some of the materials of the light love stories are taken right out of the fairy tale and the chivalric romance. For instance, the title, *A Damsel in Distress* (1919), is not as ironical as it may sound. If the heroine is not a princess, at least she is the daughter of a nobleman, and she is virtually held prisoner in a castle. Moreover, this castle has, among other residents, a cruel stepmother. The hero is a kind of congenital knight-errant who, even before he meets Lady Maud, wishes that he were living in the Middle Ages, when there were always plenty of maidens waiting to be rescued from one plight or another. In no time at all (the wish granted as though by magic) he is given an opportunity to protect Lady Maud in the streets of London. Properly modest, she keeps her identity a secret, but he later discovers it and sets out on a romantic quest to her castle in Hampshire. There he offers his services without thought of reward, though he has loved her ever since their chance meeting in London.

More recent and more important origins of the novels of love and adventure are nineteenth-century melodrama and twentieth-century crook novels. (It is significant that the Raffles stories are favorite books of Wodehouse's schoolboys.) First, the plots often turn upon questions of identity and other mysteries. There are aliases, impersonations, and disguises in profusion. In *A Gentleman of Leisure* (1910) a grafting New York policeman turns out to be an Englishman expelled from Eton and disowned for stealing. In *Something Fresh* Ashe Marson goes to Blandings Castle as a valet and Joan Valentine goes as a lady's maid. In *A Damsel in Distress* George Bevan effects his entrance into Belpher Castle by assuming the role of a temporary waiter. In *Leave It to Psmith* (1923) Psmith masquerades as the Canadian, Ralston McTodd. In scores of books that follow, countless characters, with or without false mustaches, eye patches, and the like, and for good or bad reasons, become French counts, bookies, British noblemen, American millionaires, and so on. In *If I Were You* (1931) there is a more melodramatic device involving identity. A commoner's baby and the heir to a title and a great estate are switched in their cradles.

Second, there is a concentration of the intrigue on theft. When, in the first school novel, Wodehouse introduced the robbery of the school cups, he opened up one of the main lines of his career. *A Gentleman of Leisure,* the first novel for adults after *Love Among the Chickens,* opens with the performance of a crook play and continues with breaking and entering on a bet, serious larceny, and the passing of paste jewels for genuine ones. Thereafter, Wodehouse provides a long succession of thefts: pearls, diamonds, scarabs, manuscripts, paintings are stolen, restolen, and restored by professionals and amateurs of both sexes and of all ages.

A more immediate source of the romantic novels is the musical comedy in which Wodehouse worked for a long while. Though Wodehouse is one of the most ingenious of plot-makers, the main outlines of the romantic novels are faithful to the simple shape of the conventional musical. And the approach to love is as sentimental and superficial as it usually is on the musical stage. The hero always falls in love at first sight, finding in the loved one his soul-mate (the notion of soul-mates is the only metaphysical doctrine in the whole of Wodehouse). Thus, in *Summer Moonshine* (1938), Joe Vanringham says to Jane Abbott: "We belong to each other. I knew it the moment I saw you. We were made for each other. It's only once in a lifetime that you meet anyone you can feel that about. You never get a second chance. It was a miracle, our meeting. If we throw it away, there won't be another." [1] Having met the heroine, the hero may lose sight of her (Wodehouse's version of boy loses girl), or he may find that she is either in love with another man or engaged to a man whom she does not love and being importuned by her family to marry him. If she is actually in love, she must discover flaws in her fiancé, conceal them from herself for a time, and finally admit that she has fallen out of love. The question then is whether she has grounds for breaking her engagement, but it is not necessarily a serious question. It may be that her fiancé has disclosed grave defects of character, but it may be enough to learn that he has grown fatter since she last saw him.

Having got to the second engagement, Wodehouse has got to the end of his story, the implication of which is that they lived happily ever after. He is no more interested in the problems of marriage, the responsibilities and rewards of children than the lovers are. And they are themselves rather like children, without a thought for the future except for the thought that it will be no different from the present. Packy Franklyn is perhaps less mature than the average, but not much. At the end of *Hot Water* (1932) he says to Jane Opal, "We'll just roam about the world together for the rest of our lives, raising Cain hand in hand." [2] There are plenty of people already married when the novels begin, but Wodehouse is not interested in exploring the variations of the married state, contenting himself with stereotypes. If his married couples are not close to Maggie and Jiggs, they are likely to be close to Darby and Joan. The former types predominate, since older characters are more often than not used for comic relief, and friction produces more comedy than placidity does.

Wodehouse's favorite locales for the light romantic novels (and, indeed, for the others) are, first, country houses and castles, together with their adjacent villages (pubs, inns, cottages) and, second, the world of the theater. Wodehouse keeps using these settings because he knows them well. In them he has a great deposit of inside knowledge, tradition, and trade secrets, and as a professional novelist he exploits them fully, though not realistically.

Besides, the country house and the theater are especially well suited to his inclinations and his fictional purposes, and curiously similar to the school in a number of ways. Both are isolated from the ordinary world and are (each in its own way) artificial worlds. Both involve certain routines which practically amount to ritual. In the theater there are the processes of casting, rehearsing, opening, revising on the road. In the country house there are rituals like tea on the lawn and dinner in the hall, together with functions more richly ceremonious like the hunt ball or the house party for the young master's coming of age. Both worlds are hierarchical. In the theater there is a hierarchy running from producer, director, and stars to supporting players, chorus, and keeper of the stage door. In the country house there is a pair of hierarchies, that of the servants being, if anything, more complicated and rigid than that of their masters. Joan Valentine explains to Ashe Marson how he stands, in his disguise as valet of the principal guest, as to precedence and privilege, and how the servants dine: "You come after the butler, the housekeeper, the groom of the chamber, Lord Emsworth's valet. . . . Kitchen maids and scullery maids eat in the kitchen. Chauffeurs, footmen, under-butler, pantry-boys, hall boys, odd man and steward's room footman take their meals in the Servants' Hall. . . ." [3]

The differences between the country house and the theater are obvious, but each of the two locales appeals to a side of Wodehouse, and the contrasts between the two serve him well. The quiet, dignity, and security of the country-house atmosphere sustain him, and the precariousness, brashness, and glamour of the theater stimulate him. In each world he finds a supply of useful character types. In the country house and village there are lords, butlers, idle sons, curates, barmaids, gardeners. In the theater there are mad or bright writers, drunk actors, eccentric producers, beautiful chorus girls. Moreover, there are countless opportunities for mixing up the two kinds of character, and as Wodehouse increases the accent on comedy, he takes greater and greater advantage of the incongruities between them.

II   *The Heroes*

The heroes of the romantic novels descend on one side from the heroes of the school novels. In their middle twenties, they are not much older than boys in the upper forms, and some of them are still fond of ragging, practical jokes, and general schoolboy raffishness. Indeed, some of them are fonder of such stuff than the schoolboys are. Joe Vanringham phones the publisher for whom he works and tells him that he has gone to the wrong railway station and missed the firm's best-selling and most temperamental novelist. After the publisher has moaned and cursed for some minutes, Joe tells the truth: he has met the novelist and sent her off with candy and flowers, happy as a clam. Joe's behavior sometimes goes even further back to boyhood. Staying at Walsingford Hall, he discovers on the first day that the stone wall on the terrace is dotted with busts of the Caesars. Immediately he draws a mustache on the nearest one, and thereafter, in his free moments, he works his way methodically down the line.

In all essential matters the heroes follow the specifications of the school code. Thus, they firmly believe in the cult of games and fitness over intellect and scholarship. Though out of school and off the playing fields, they play English sports when they can, and a number of them keep in shape by doing something called Larsen's exercises. Ashe Marson is a specimen with all of the points well developed. He has a degree from Oxford, but an acceptably weak one. When the novel opens, he is living in London and doing hackwork for magazines. The reader first sees him as he emerges from his rooms into Arundel Street. "He was a tall, well-built, fit-looking young man, with a clear eye and a strong chin; and he was dressed . . . in a sweater, flannel trousers, and rubber-soled gymnasium shoes. In one hand he bore a pair of Indian clubs, in the other a skipping rope." [4] Not all of the young men, to be sure, appear with such paraphernalia, but many of them are former athletes, and all of them are athletic types. When they are not particularly tall, they still have the jaunty carriage and the deep chest of the athlete. If nothing else, they are strong, healthy animals; indeed, Wodehouse often compares them to some sort of animal. The big Wally Mason is like a large, shaggy dog, and the merely medium-sized Jimmy Pitt, with his square, slightly protruding jaw and his piercing brown eyes, is like a bull terrier.

If anything, the young men of the romances are more virile than the athletes of the school stories. They may be good-looking, but they must not be downright handsome, for that would be effeminate. As the books go on, their very names become manlier than those of the school heroes. In 1906 a hero may be called Jeremy Garnet; and in 1915 one may be called Ashe Marson (which is at least better than the pseudonym that he uses for his magazine stories, Felix Clovelly); but in 1938 he must be called something like Joe, Joss, or Sam. Any old reader of Wodehouse would guess that George Bevan is the hero of *A Damsel in Distress* and that Geoffrey Raymond is his unsuccessful rival.

As a good schoolboy does, at least in theory, the young fellows in the light romantic novels carry the code of sportsmanship into situations beyond the playing field and the school walls. Jimmy Pitt would no more think of deserting his partner in his breaking and entering for a bet (though he has known him for only a day) than Adair would think of letting the cricket side down. Tony Bryce, the nominal Earl of Droitwich, considers that it is unsporting of his family to put the real Earl through a course of painful training for nobility so as to discourage him from prosecuting his claim to the title. Hence, he explains to Syd Price that going to art galleries, riding to hounds, and wearing uncomfortable clothes are not matters of *noblesse oblige*. (As they will not bully, they will not be bullied, and they are capable of violence in defense of their rights and of good causes. "If you put a hand on me," Jimmy Pitt tells the corrupt police captain McEachern, "I'll finish you. . . . Do you think I care for your size?" [5]) No less dependable in routine situations than in critical ones, many of the young men do dull jobs with the cheerful spirit of a good cricketer getting up for fielding practice before breakfast.

Ultimately, however, the heroes of the romantic novels are modeled less on Mike and the other athletes of the school stories than they are on Psmith. For one thing, they are all nonstop talkers, and some of their favorite phrases, axioms, and cracks are Psmith's. Threatened with a punch in the nose if he tries to get into the cab where Lady Maud is hiding, Percy Belpher tells

George Bevan that people do not do such things, that it is impossible. George's reply is exactly the one that Psmith makes to another schoolboy who says that it is impossible for a new boy to take possession of a room that an old boy wants: "We must distinguish between the unusual and the impossible." [6] But the romantic heroes improve upon Psmith's diction, as Psmith himself does when he appears in an adult book, making it brisker and less pedantic. In *Psmith in the City* Psmith makes a page-long speech and then adds, "I am a poor, unready speaker, but I intend to acquire a knowledge of the Law which shall outweigh this defect." [7] In *Leave It to Psmith* he says to a member of his club who is incensed that Psmith has given away his umbrella to a pretty girl whom he saw in the street: ". . . I selected it as the only possible one from a number of competitors. I fear this club is becoming very mixed. . . . You with your pure mind would hardly believe the rottenness of some of the umbrellas I inspected in the cloak-room." [8]

In most cases the romantic heroes are as irreverent to authority as Psmith is. Joss Weatherby bumptiously sits in his boss's chair, orders his secretary around, and announces that tycoons appear to have an easy life. Other young blades worry and taunt their employers out of pure high spirits or lack of other amusement. Like Psmith, they have a talent for getting other people to do things for them. Weatherby goes to a country house in the guise of a valet, but he does not live the life of a servant. By a combination of nerve, fast talk, and money, he manages to have the other servants do his work and to make himself comfortable into the bargain. He has a good room with a bath; a kitchen maid brings him his morning cup of tea; the cook sees that there are sandwiches on his bedside table at night; and the butler makes sure that there is whisky and soda to go with them. A footman does most of the valeting.

Newer developments are partly derived from the experiences of the young Wodehouse just after Dulwich and from the experiences of friends whom he met in this period. Recently out of school, the heroes are now on their own. Versatile and resourceful, they get along by turning their hands to all manner of jobs, some of them, like Wodehouse himself, writing for magazines. Before he comes into money, even Jimmy Pitt has been newspaperman, boxer, actor, waiter, and jeweler's assistant. Joe Vanringham has been sailor on tramp steamers, bouncer, and editor. As late as *Summer Moonshine* there is a hero who leaves home at twenty-one, with only ten dollars to his name, and makes his way in the world. Independence remains a cardinal virtue to Wodehouse for a long while. It is only after he has made himself rich by hard work that he inclines to make his heroes either rich by inheritance or parasites upon the rich. Then they are likely to be members of the Drones Club, brushing elbows at the bar with such fellows as Catsmeat Potter-Pirbright, only a step away from being heroes of farce instead of heroes of romance.

What is altogether new in the evolution of the school-story hero into the hero of the romantic novels is, of course, the interest in girls. To this interest most of them (unlike the knightly George Bevan) bring the same bold, brash, unconscionable qualities that they bring to bosses. "I tell you, young Jane," one of them says, "it is hopeless for you to try to escape me. You are as good as walking up the aisle already. You shake your head? Just you wait. A time will come—and that shortly—when you will be doing so in order to dislodge the deposits of rice and confetti which have gathered in your lovely hair." [9] Confident though they may profess to be, they will resort to anything to make assurance doubly sure. Sam Marlowe mugs up Billie Bennett's tastes and finds that she is a lover of dogs, golf, and *The Idylls of the King*. An honest lover of the first two himself, he pretends to have a passion for Tennyson, of whom he has never read any more than he was compelled to. To look brave before the girl, he tells her that a mild law clerk is a homocidal maniac, thus frightening her half to death.

Yet these lovers are as devoted as they are determined, as humble as they are impudent. The man who tells a girl that she is inevitably going to fall in love with him will accept rejection without a murmur and then tell her that if she should ever change her mind, he will come running. When finally accepted, he can scarcely believe in his good fortune: ". . . I have this crushing sense of unworthiness. If someone came along at this moment and said, 'Tell me, Weatherby, to settle a bet, what have you done to deserve this?' I should be nonplussed. I shouldn't know what to answer. I should just go all red and shuffle my feet." [10]

The attitude toward women is, indeed extraordinarily reverent, pure, and innocent. A woman is half goddess and half child, a figure to inspire both awe and a feeling of protection. On page 164 of *Something Fresh* Ashe Marson is still calling Joan "Miss Valentine." Still later in the same novel another young man addresses a twenty-year-old woman as "little girl." [11] Successful, rich, famous, surrounded by beautiful girls, George Bevan is as modest and unspoiled, as morally immaculate as he was when (like the young Wodehouse) he hung around theaters, hoping to be given the job of interpolating a number in a show. A tougher hero than George fears that he has put himself beyond the pale when he instinctively seizes the heroine, hugs, and kisses her. For he has committed the unforgivable sin, "taking advantage of a helpless girl." [12]

The characters of the suitors whom the heroes replace are drawn in accord with a few simple principles of contrast. Since it is one of the axioms of the Wodehouse world that a hero must be fit, no overweight man can be considered a serious suitor or a formidable rival. Neither can any effeminate man. In Wodehouse's novels some of the earmarks of this type are a willowy build, butter-colored hair, delicate good looks (sometimes marred by a large Adam's apple), perfect manners, a minor talent for playing the piano, and the habit of singing "Trees" after dinner. Another ineligible type is the man dependent on and fearful of his relatives or trustees (though he is innocuous and is qualified to be a comic hero). But a man may have independence, virility, and the right weight, and still be the worst type of all, the cad. In Wodehouse even the cad does not seduce girls (nobody does), but he breaks engagements.

Though the self-respecting man is not obliged to horsewhip the cad, he should have nothing to do with him. To Freddie Rooke, who does not seem to understand this, Wally Mason explains: "You're a public school man. You've mixed all the time with decent people. You wouldn't do anything that wasn't straight yourself to save your life. Yet it seems to have made absolutely no difference in your opinion of this man Underhill that he behaved like an utter cad to a girl who was one of your best friends." [13] When Underhill rejects Jill a *second* time, after learning that she has lost her money and become a chorus girl, Freddie perceives that he is no good and tells him off: "I've always looked up to you . . . and wished I was like you, but, Great Scott! If that's the sort of chap you are, I'm deuced glad I'm not. . . . If we ever meet again I'll trouble you not to speak to me, because I've a reputation to keep up. So there you have it in a bally nutshell." [14] Algy Martyn tells Underhill that from now on he and all of his friends, both men and women, will cut him. Though Freddie and Algy speak in the idiom of the Drones Club and their I. Q.'s are, if anything, lower than the Drones's average (their names are a tip-off to their intelligence), at least they know right from wrong.

III *Heroines*

The young women of the romances are of about the same age as the young men, that is, about as old as boys in their third or fourth year out of school, and their characters and way of looking at the world are roughly those of the young men. Either they have learned or they have grasped instinctively the elements of a code that is essentially the school code. You cannot, for example, lie directly when forced to a yes or no (on the other hand, it is unsporting of authority to force one to a yes or no), but it is all right to evade and temporize. Having learned that Lady Maud, pressed by her family, has thus evaded and then revealed the truth, George Bevan considers it another proof of what a fine woman she is. The conception of duty is also a kind of school loyalty and stoical good sportsmanship. Whatever his flaws may be, they will not break an engagement to a man who actually needs them. They place a great value on courage, do not panic in crises, and take their losses well. When they weep, they do so briefly and unobtrusively. "She fought the devils and she routed the devils, till presently a final sniff told that the battle had been won. Shropshire, which had been a thing of mist, became firmer in its outlines. She put away the handkerchief and stood blinking defiantly." [15]

Like the young men, many of the young women are making their own way in the world. Lady Maud is not, but at least she does not *look* like an aristocrat. Her nose is very nearly patrician, but it tilts slightly at the tip after the Wodehouse model, and she has the usual determined little chin. Jill Mariner is a rich girl, but not for long, since her fool of an uncle loses her money. Most of the girls have never had any easy pickings, and their names are appropriately simple and ordinary: Sally, Sue, Polly, Molly, and so on. Always they are small, slender, dynamic types (statuesque women are either tyrannical or comic). They scamper about like kittens; and when they accept proposals, the young men pick them up and swing them off their feet, asking them if they weigh about five pounds.

If the men are cheerful, the girls are appallingly so. Eve Halliday's former schoolmistress remarks that Eve has had a hard life, and Eve admits it but then says that it has been a lark and that she has loved every minute of it. They are also aggressively kind and protective. One of them calls a strike when a girl in her theatrical troupe is unjustly fired. Another is in the habit of asking waiters about their lumbago and valets about their chillblains. She helps push the cart of an overloaded horse in Bond Street and reprimands a man who is harassing a parrot with a stick.

For all their cheerful resilience and their championship of the weak, the heroines have something of the old-fashioned girl in them. They still like to cling occasionally and to be petted (which in Wodehouse means to have their hands patted). The working girls, making their way through the jungle of the city, yearn for a more idyllic existence. "What I ought to have done," says one of the show girls, "was to buy a gingham bonnet and milk cows. My father was a nursery gardener out in Indiana. . . . I used to hang about Covent Garden . . . The boys that mess about with the flowers there . . . got to look on me as part of the scenery." [16] Whatever their occupation or lack of one, the girls are as pure as those in Victorian novelettes. They are able to go through the perilous world by themselves, partly because they are, like Shakespeare's Rosaline, "in strong proof of chastity well armed," and partly because they always suspect the worst. Embraced and kissed by the gentlest hero in the books, one of them exclaims indignantly, "I didn't think you were—that kind of man." [17]

IV *From Romance to Farce*

The romantic novels are clearly not the strongest part of Wodehouse's work, but even at their weakest they have their points. If the characters are uncomplicated and immature, at least they have the refreshing high spirits of youth. If the world in which they live has some rather absurd Victorian elements in it, it also has a kind of period charm. If the books have no great depths, their surfaces sparkle frequently enough with the exuberance of language that is one of Wodehouse's most attractive qualities. At their best they are nearly as entertaining as the pure comedies since, as they become better and better, they come closer and closer to the comedies. They have a number of astringent ingredients to counteract their sentimentality, and with the years these grow stronger.

At a fairly early stage the adventure in the romantic novels is played more for laughter than for melodramatic thrills. Necklaces, portraits, and manuscripts are pinched within the family and at the behest of the heroine, just as in the Bertie Wooster novels they are pinched at the behest of Aunt Dahlia. Frequently they are pinched only so that they may be returned and the thief ingratiated with the owner. Furthermore, the nature of the swag changes, so that not only diamonds and rare silver are stolen, but also pet dogs and prize pigs.

The larcenous themes are played with all the stops of farce out. The thief endures midnight vigils under drawing-room windows while beetles fall down his neck. Entire households assemble in their nightclothes and run around shouting. In the dark of country houses people crash into each other and trip over dogs and cats. Wodehouse particularly likes to have someone come tumbling down a staircase and into a small table which, with the many china ornaments invariably placed on it, is smashed with a most satisfactory noise. He also likes to lock people in coal cellars and potting sheds, trap them on roofs or the ledges of upper-story windows, and tree them in the noble oaks of great estates. Even Psmith, who, of all of Wodehouse's heroes, comes closest to playing the role of Raffles, overcomes a gunman with farcical assistance. Bound and gagged in a second-floor room of a cottage, Freddie Threepwood thrashes around and sticks his foot through the flimsy ceiling, thus providing the distraction that Psmith needs.

The romance, too, is invaded by comedy. First, the comic foils displace some of the room taken up by the leads and become major characters. Lord Emsworth, for instance, begins as a stock type of absent-minded old man and eventually becomes the center of a series. Albert Peasemarch, the long-winded and officious ship's steward, thrusts and talks his way into a prominent position in the Wodehouse world as he thrusts and talks his way into staterooms. The silly young asses, who function as companions, rivals, and reflectors of the heroes, begin to function in their own right, as they do so magnificently in the farces. Sometimes the main love affair is itself treated in terms of farce. One hero, having hidden in a suit of armor, is unable to get the helmet off and has to propose in it, driving around with his girl in a roadster for half the night until she accepts him.

Even when Wodehouse is being ostensibly romantic, he kids romance. For instance, he likes to draw comparisons between the situations in the novels and earlier ones. To avoid compromising a young woman, a young man flees from her room to a balcony. To this same balcony, Wodehouse tells the reader, an eighteenth-century lord once fled for the same purpose, minutes later leaping from it with brave abandon. An obvious invocation, one might suppose, of a more gallant age to enhance the character of the hero. But in the conclusion of the scene the hero does not become a gallant, but a clown. Instead of leaping from the balcony like his predecessor, he climbs to the window above on sheets lowered to him by a raffish page boy. A few novels later the kidding by parallel becomes broader, and the sources of the parallels are discovered in the lower levels of fiction. The valet Webster compares the problem of the lover in *The Girl on the Boat* (1922) to that of the lover in *Cupid or Mammon,* a volume in the Nosegay Novelette Series. In the course of suggesting various stratagems by which the young man might find his way out of the difficulty, he also draws four or five parallels from other volumes in the series. Finally, he recommends that the young man kidnap his girl's dog, as the hero kidnapped the younger brother of the heroine in *Footpaths of Fate.*

Wodehouse uses the diction of the sentimental novel with similar irony. "He clasped her to his bosom and showered burning kisses upon her upturned face," [18] he says when Joss and Sally embrace near the conclusion of *Quick Service* (1940). If the reader should imagine that Wodehouse is quite serious, he learns otherwise when, in the last lines of the book, Wodehouse uses exactly the same words to describe the embrace (in reconciliation after fierce squabbling) of a pair of comic characters already married: the illiterate, third-rate boxer, Howard Steptoe, and the wealthy Mrs. Steptoe.

As early as 1922, Wodehouse is joking about the very cornerstones of the romantic novel. Girls like Jane Hubbard (whom Wodehouse compares to the young Boadicia), athletes, big-game hunters, and the like, are initially introduced as foils for the very feminine heroines. But Jane, for one, also serves to make fun of the convention of the manly man and the womanly woman. Eventually, she says, she would like to quit big-game hunting and go into Parliament. "And if I did that, I should practically have to marry. I mean I should have to have a man to look after the social end of life and arrange parties and receptions and so on, and sit ornamentally at my table . . . When I came back a bit done up after a long sitting at the House, he would mix me a whisky and soda and read poetry to me or prattle about all the things he had been doing during the day. . . ." [19]

As for the romantic heroines themselves, a number of them become as silly as the girls in the comic novels. At the opening of *The Girl on the Boat* Billie Bennett, in her quest for her "ideal," her "knight," has got engaged three times in three weeks. She thinks that she has at last found her knight in Sam Marlowe, but she is immediately disenchanted when Sam makes a fool of himself at a ship's concert. (Her original impression of heroism was equally ill-founded. Sam did not dive off the ship to rescue a drowning man; the man was an excellent swimmer, and Sam was pushed.) Billie even speaks the bird-brained dialogue of Madeline Bassett, the cursed girl who blights the life of Augustus Fink-Nottle. After Sam proposes to her, she confesses that she once thought that Eustace Hignett was her ideal. "Eustace and . . . you!" snorts Sam indignantly. "The Princess and the Swineherd." "Does Mr. Hignett keep pigs?" [20] Billie asks in surprise.

Finally, though the point of the romantic novels is to get the lovers to the threshold of what will presumably be a marriage happy ever after, there is a picture to contend with that of wedded bliss: the picture of bachelor contentment. When the comic foil to the hero discovers that he has lost the girl, his first feeling is disappointment, but his subsequent feeling is relief. And his relief is transformed to elation when his father or his guardian agrees to restore his allowance so that he can live in London in a bachelor flat. Freddie Threepwood, for example, is not the hero of *Something Fresh*, but he is cut from the same cloth as the hero of the best novels that Wodehouse has written, the series about Bertie Wooster.

CHAPTER 5

Comedy

I *The Young Comedians*

IN THE last sixty years, Wodehouse has written so much comedy that thousands of readers must think of him as a comic writer only. The clown Ukridge first appeared in 1906; Lord Emsworth and his son Freddie appeared in 1915. Thereafter the comedians increased and multiplied, and by the 1920's they had become not only stooges but also protagonists. The immortal Bertie Wooster himself made his debut in a short story in 1917. But Wodehouse was torn two ways for a long while. As late as 1940 Wodehouse's hero may be a romantic of the first water; it is only in the last twenty-five years that the Berties and the Pongos, the Bingos and the Tuppys have dominated Wodehouse's world. Readers may regret that it took Wodehouse so much time to get from the wholesome but prankish schoolboy to the romantic and heroic young man to the bumbling and unheroic figure of the pure comedies; but this figure would not have been possible without the preparation of the earlier ones.

Comedy is Wodehouse's greatest achievement, and his comic heroes are his main contribution to the mythology of popular literature. Like the romantic heroes, the comic ones have attended good schools and universities; but we may surmise that they are not the products of the great and ancient seats of learning, but the rejects. The career of Freddie Threepwood is somewhat more inglorious than the average, but not much more. Freddie did not even get through Eton, having been expelled for breaking out at night and roaming the streets of Windsor in a false mustache. Later, he was sent down from Oxford for pouring ink from a second-story window on the dean of his college. He spent the next two years with an expensive crammer, but still failed to pass into the Army. When he is introduced in *Something Fresh*, he has accumulated a stack of debts and a cluster of shady friends, most of them connected with horse racing. At his preparatory school, Gussie Fink-Nottle was called "fathead," a nickname of more than ordinary significance because his competitors were such dolts as Freddie Widgeon. Charles Edward Biffen must have the shortest memory span on record. Grown to man's estate, Biffy is wandering around Paris, lost, when he runs into Bertie Wooster.

"Bertie!" he gurgled in a devout sort of tone. "Thank God." He clutched my arm. "Don't leave me, Bertie. I'm lost."

"What do you mean, lost?"

"I came out for a walk and suddenly discovered after a mile or two that I didn't know where on earth I was. I've been wandering around in circles for hours."

"Why didn't you ask the way?"

"I can't speak a word of French."

"Well, why didn't you call a taxi?"

"I suddenly discovered I'd left all my money at my hotel."

"You could have taken a cab and paid it when you got to the hotel."

"Yes, but I suddenly discovered, dash it, that I'd forgotten its name." [1]

Biffy is even capable of forgetting the name of a girl to whom he has proposed. One and all, the comic heroes are about as feeble in talent and enterprise as they are in intelligence. When they brood, they gaze into space with glassy eyes and chew the knobs of their canes. When they have leisure for self-improvement, they try to balance umbrellas on the tips of their noses. When they wish to contribute to the gaiety of nations, they do an imitation of a bull-terrier chasing a cat up a tree or, alternatively, a bulldog fighting a Pekinese.

Unlike the romantic fellows, the comedians are often dependent on their parents, uncles, and aunts. (Bingo Little goes from dependence on his uncle to dependence on his wife, Rosie Banks, a famous writer of profitable gooey fiction, who confines him to an allowance for cigarettes.) In consequence, they are always looking for ways of making money. Sometimes, implausibly, they get temporary jobs as tutors or journalists, but they prefer activities less arduous though more risky. Bingo, for example, pawns his cuff links and then finds himself in jeopardy because his wife, thinking that they are stolen, wants the police to check the pawn-shops. Their favorite source of income is gambling, and their favorite form of gambling is playing the horses, but they contrive to bet on more things than horses. At the Drones Club there is a fat uncles sweepstakes. Stuck in the country for a time, several characters run a sweepstakes on the length of the sermons to be preached by clergymen in nearby villages. The clowns are not above conspiracy and betting on a sure thing. Oofy Prosser, the pimpled millionaire of the Drones Club (an exception in wealth though not in intelligence) arranges for Bingo Little, as judge in a baby contest, to award the prize to his own son, entered as Oofy's nephew. Compounding the fraud, Oofy phones a wager on the baby to his bookmaker. Since he tells the bookmaker that the baby resembles himself, he gets very good odds.

The young comedians are repressed and harassed by mothers, fathers, and uncles, but mostly by aunts, who are the very scourge of youth, and who appear to have increased in geometrical progression from the earliest books to the latest. In 1906 Ukridge has a couple of aunts, one of them by marriage, but in 1949 Esmond Haddock has five aunts, all by blood and all dreadful. In a free-association test given to Wodehouse's nephews, any word indicating unpleasantness would probably have "aunt" as a response. Certainly nephews associate unpleasant *objects* with aunts. Suffering from a hangover and gazing at a badly poached egg, one nephew complains that it looks like an aunt of his. Another, regarding a house with disapproval, says that it is the kind of house that an aunt would live in.

Like the romantic heroes, the comic ones are greatly attracted to girls. If they win them, they go around with their hats on the side of their heads. If they lose them, they brood (one sits moodily at the piano by the hour, playing "The Rosary" with one finger). They are, nevertheless, very dubious about the serious commitment of marriage. Even a hero like Monty Bodkin, who is in transition from the romantic to the comic, fears that his fiancée is too earnest a girl. "It's an unpleasant thing to say about anyone, but the fact of the matter is, Gertrude's the soul of honor." [2] The Montys no more want to have responsibility for others than they want others to have authority over them. As Packy Franklyn watches a group of fathers and children at Waterloo Station, the fathers all seem to wear a worried look which proclaims their regret at ever marrying. The barber Meech in *If I Were You* is a bachelor, but he sometimes has an air of melancholy which can only be described as the look of a married man.

Hence bachelorhood can compete with marriage on at least even terms. Freddie Rooke's rooms are very cozy against the London chill, and his man Barker slips softly about the place like Bertie's Jeeves. The club, too, often looks more attractive than the vine-covered cottage. In the club, young men can be in an entirely masculine society as they were at school, and they can rag and row as they did at school (at least in some clubs: at the Drones there is a good deal of bread-throwing in the dining room). Besides, they can do on a large scale what they could scarcely do at all in school: they can drink. When Monty asks Reggie Tennyson whether he has a headache, Reggie replies, "My dear fellow, last night the Drones gave me a farewell party with Catsmeat Potter-Pirbright in the chair. Need I say more?" [3]

II *Bertie Wooster*

Wodehouse's crowning achievement in the creation of the silly young ass is Bertie Wooster, the ideal Drone. First of all, though not so stupid as Biffy, he is not much more intelligent (by Jeeves's estimate, his intellect is negligible). The one piece of sustained mental work that he does during his adult life leaves him completely exhausted. After finishing an article on "What the Well-Dressed Man is Wearing" for his Aunt Dahlia's paper, "I blotted the last page of my manuscript, feeling more or less a spent force." [4]

Second, Bertie is extremely indolent. It is unlikely that at school he ever got up to train with the keen boys before breakfast. Now, certainly, he breakfasts in bed or at least stays there until Jeeves brings him a cup of tea or possibly one of his mixtures for hangovers. He sleeps nine hours a night and supplements this rest with frequent sessions in an armchair during the day. Gradually he has left most of his enthusiasm for athletics behind him. At some village sports contest or other he won the choir boys' handicap race; he was a Racquet Blue at Oxford; and he still plays golf. In an emergency, he can get off the mark briskly enough, sprinting from the police in a gambling raid or engaging in a spot of commando fighting in a country house. But it is more usual for him to get his exercise by strolling through Bond Street. As a spectator and bettor, however, he still has considerable interest in sport. He is inclined to talk of the likelihood of anything in terms of odds, as if he were at the track, and he remembers important occasions by associating them with races. For instance, he recalls that his Aunt Dahlia married his Uncle Tom in the same year that Bluebottle won the Cambridge.

Third, Bertie is a great eater and drinker. It is only the thought of being cut off from the cooking of Aunt Dahlia's chef, Anatole, that gives Bertie the courage to undertake some of Aunt Dahlia's mad commissions. As for drinking, Aunt Dahlia tells him that every time she sees him, he appears to be "recovering from some debauch. Don't you ever stop drinking? How about when you're asleep?" [5] Bertie insists that he drinks a lot only on special occasions, like boat-race night or a supper for a man about to be married. Ordinarily, he says, his drinking is moderate: a brace of cocktails, wine with dinner, and a liqueur after it. The numerous whiskies and sodas mixed by himself or by Jeeves, by day or by night, have slipped his mind.

Bertie has a sufficient appreciation of feminine charms (the beauty of Pauline Stoker, he says, "maddened me like wine" [6]), but he is one of nature's bachelors. The point of the Wooster stories and novels, therefore, is the opposite of that of the romantic novels, not to get the hero married, but to keep him single. Aunt Dahlia, whose brain sometimes works on the sporting lines of Bertie's, wishes that she had five pounds for every time that Bertie has been only a step away from the altar and still managed to escape. For a while Bertie may believe that he is inconsolable, but then he comes to feel that he is well out of marriage, and eventually he decides that there is nothing so exhilarating as finding that you do not have to be married after all.

The girls that Bertie is involved with, whether or not they wish to marry him, are invariably beautiful, but they differ in other respects, the first type being the wild ones. They rather resemble in temperament some of the less inhibited schoolboys and, as Richard Usborne remarks, they often have names that could be boys' as well as girls' names. [7] Evidently some of them have an epicene look. When he introduces Bobbie Wickham, Wodehouse says that she is an extraordinarily beautiful girl, but he also says that she resembles a very good-looking schoolboy dressed in his sister's clothes. The wild girls also resemble some of the wild young men. Having lost her shirt on a race, Emerald Stoker (the sister of Pauline) takes a job as a cook in a country house to tide her over until her next check from her father. (Though he is a millionaire, if he found out that she had been gambling, there would be the devil to pay and the end of her allowance.) In spite of such similarities and in spite of the initial description of Bobbie Wickham, the loveliness of the girls is certifiably feminine. In a later description of Bobbie herself, Wodehouse says, "Her outer crust was . . . of a nature to cause those beholding it to rock back on their heels with a startled whistle. . . . She was equipped with eyes like twin stars, hair ruddier than the cherry, oomph, *espièglerie*, and all the fixings." [8]

The wild young women compel young men to puncture people's hot water bottles, push constables in ponds, steal, kidnap, and so on. Sometimes these customary crimes have a purpose, and sometimes they are done just for the hell of it. Thus, Pauline Stoker, having hidden out in Bertie Wooster's rented cottage, dressed in his pyjamas, and got into his bed, suggests that Bertie pour water out of the window on her stern father below. In the first Bobbie Wickham story, the magistrate, Sir Joseph Moresby, fines Bobbie for speeding and calls her "a red-headed hussy who ought to be smacked and sent to bed without her supper." [9] For once, Bertie would agree with a magistrate, as his remarks on a similar girl suggest: "The whole fact of the matter is that all this modern emancipation of women has resulted in them getting it up their noses and not giving a damn what they do. It was not like this in Queen Victoria's day. The Prince Consort would have had a word to say about a girl like Stiffy, what?" [10]

A second kind of girl is overpowering in a very different way. Because she is earnest, she wishes to reform Bertie, to make him drink and smoke less, for instance. Because she is intelligent, she wishes to educate him, to make him read Bergson and go to serious plays instead of musical comedies. Because she is athletic, she wishes to get him into condition. Bertie discovers that Honoria Glossop, for instance, is the kind of girl who would run him ragged on the tennis court all afternoon and then expect him to talk intelligently about Freud at dinner. Such a girl has too much virtue for Bertie, and though she has a perfect profile, she is too active for him to be able to see her standing sideways much of the time.

The third type of girl is the sappy. Dismayed by the Honoria Glossops and the Florence Crayes, Bertie says that he prefers a girl on the Janet Gaynor model, one who clings and prattles; he is pleased to stroke the hand of such a girl and murmur a few comforting words in her ear. But the sappy girls go too far. Madeline Bassett believes that the stars are God's daisy chain and that the mists over the meadows are the bridal veils of the elves. Phyllis Mills speaks in baby talk, asking Bertie if he does not think that the dachshund Poppet is a sweet little doggie and asserting that Bertie's friend Kipper Herring is a lambkin. Of all the silly girls Madeline is the worst. She has got it into her head that Bertie loves her, and whenever she breaks her engagement to Gussie Fink-Nottle, she turns to Bertie.

Bound by the code of the Woosters, Bertie is not allowed to disenchant her, so that in several novels he is very nearly caught in Madeline's gooey embrace. In her fatuous way, Madeline sees in Bertie's supposed love an equivalent of that of the hero in one of the slushy novels by Rosie Banks, like *Mervyn Keene, Clubman*. Wodehouse is, of course, making fun not only of the tradition of sentimental fiction, but also of his own earlier romantic novels in which the chivalrous hero was always ready to come running back if the girl broke her engagement to her first lover. Nowhere in the world, apparently, is there a soul-mate for Bertie, but if he ever should get married and have a son, he knows what he will name him: Green Swizzle Wooster, after a West Indian drink that saved him from death by thirst, fatigue, and boredom during a tour of the British Empire Exhibition at Wembley.

Bertie's two aunts give him as much trouble as all of the girls put together. So sorely do his aunts beset him that he once tells Jeeves that if he had his life to live over again, he would start it without aunts. Wistfully he thinks how, in Turkey, aunts were put in sacks and dropped into the Bosporus, until Jeeves explains that odalisques, not aunts, were thus disposed of. The worse of the two aunts is Agatha, the one who, Bertie says, kills rats with her teeth and wears barbed wire next to the skin. Aunt Agatha is an older Honoria Glossop, a woman who wants to turn Bertie into a serious and responsible man, failing to see that the operation is painful and the change in any case, impossible.

Bertie, however, wins one or two small victories over Aunt Agatha and at last he evidently defies her. After Esmond Haddock has told off his five aunts, Bertie is emboldened by his example. Instead of doing what he has done so often before, climbing out of a window and down a water pipe to take the milk train to London, he strides bravely to Aunt Agatha's door. In the last lines of *The Mating Season* (1949) he tells how, poised at the door he feels like Childe Roland ready to fight the Paynim. Whether this mood of resolution prevailed in the face of the dreadful Aunt Agatha, we cannot, of course, be certain. We can speculate, however, what the odds at the Drones Club might be.

Though Aunt Dahlia lands Bertie in many a disaster, she is the one whom he calls, in an amiable echo of Dickens and the Victorian age, his aged relative and his deserving aunt. He can get along better with Dahlia than with Agatha because he has much in common with her. She criticizes his drinking, but she is fond enough of the bottle herself, and her chef Anatole is, after all, the best in the United Kingdom. But if Aunt Agatha is an Honoria Glossop grown older, Aunt Dahlia is a Stephanie Byng grown older. She may have fewer scruples than anyone in the books except Ukridge. Until she sold *Milady's Boudoir* to a chump from Liverpool, she kept it afloat by extracting periodic sums from Uncle Tom on false pretenses. She does not stick at bribing, and stealing, much of it delegated to the reluctant Bertie, on pain of exclusion from her dining room.

Aunt Dahlia's favorite device, however, is blackmail, the value of which she discovered when still a slip of a girl: she saw Bertie's Uncle George kissing her governess, and she held the event over his head whenever he made a move to punish her. Before the period of the books, Aunt Dahlia was a great fox hunter, and the bugle voice that she developed by shouting over the fields has sometimes come near shattering Bertie's ear drums. She also retains the vocabulary of the hunting field, and Bertie frequently censors her talk for the sake of the reader. In the crises of her life she is easily moved to violent action, relieving her emotions by breaking, treading on, or smashing against the wall whatever small and fragile object happens to be nearest.

Besides Aunts, Bertie has a number of other troubles. Conspicuous on the list is Sir Roderick Glossop, the father of Honoria. Sir Roderick is widely known as a nerve specialist, but Bertie repeatedly assures the reader that he is no more than a wily fellow with a practice confined to the dotty rich. Bertie has never been a patient of Sir Roderick, but Sir Roderick thinks that he ought to be and, convinced that Bertie is a certifiable lunatic, he tries to convince others. He first began to doubt Bertie's sanity when, at Lady Wickham's country house, Bertie sneaked into his bedroom and punctured his hot water bottle. (Bertie did so at the instigation of Bobbie Wickham and in the belief that the room was that of Sir Roderick's nephew, Tuppy Glossop.) Since then, Sir Roderick has often turned up at critical junctures in Bertie's life, each time to find what looks to him like further proof of Bertie's madness (for instance, collections of fish, cats, and stolen top hats left in Bertie's bedroom by practical-joking friends).

Another ancient enemy of Bertie's is the Reverend Aubrey Upjohn, headmaster of Bertie's preparatory school, Malvern House. Bertie is pleased (and amazed) to discover that since school days Upjohn has become less terrifying. At school, says Bertie, Upjohn was "about eight feet in height, with burning eyes, foam-flecked lips, and flame coming out from both nostrils. He had now shrunk to a modest five foot seven or thereabouts, and I could have felled him with a single blow." [11] However much he has diminished physically, Upjohn has retained all of his old moral strength, and Bertie finds it difficult to stand up to him, even over the long-distance telephone. Face to face, he is still frightening enough, with his long, bare upper lip and an expression (one gathers) like that of the actor, Henry Danielle, in one of his sadistic roles.

Then there is a cluster of miscellaneous enemies that includes every magistrate in England, starting with Sir Watkyn Bassett, who twice in one year fined his own niece, Stiffy Byng, for speeding. Bertie has a theory that magistrates get rich by pocketing the fines that they impose on their victims; over the years, the shillings are bound to mount up. The private soldiers of the enemy are constables. At the conclusion of *The Code of the Woosters* (1938) Bertie's happiness is complete when he realizes that Constable Oates, whom Sir Watkyn forgot to dismiss, is walking guard under the windows to prevent Bertie's escape, while the rain comes down by the bucket. Other enemies are young fellows who imagine that Bertie has designs on their fiancées, especially when these fellows are great gorillas like Roderick Spode.

Also in the camp of the enemy are small boys, who often look like gangsters and who, when they are not doing something worse, patronize Bertie. Once Bertie, after traveling all night on milk trains between the country and London, blear-eyed, disheveled, unshaved, encounters one such boy, who gives him a penny and tells him not to spend it on drink. Even the animal kingdom includes some beasts who prey on Bertie. Stiffy Byng's Aberdeen terrier, Bartholomew, not only takes pieces out of Bertie's leg but, having treed him on a bureau, looks at him from under beetling brows, like a Scotch elder rebuking sinners. An angry swan pursues Bertie and forces him to climb to the roof of a boathouse. Finally, Bertie's friends and Bertie himself are enemies. For when called upon to assist old friends, in whatever fantastic endeavors and at whatever risk to himself, Bertie must, in accord with the code of the Woosters, do so.

From all perils Bertie is defended by his valet Jeeves, who is everything that Bertie is not. In these two contrasting characters, Wodehouse discovered the perfect expression of his comic talents, and they are as much the major figures in his work as Sherlock Holmes and Doctor Watson are in Doyle's. Jeeves's erudition exceeds Holmes's. He has not only English but also Latin literature (in the original) at his fingertips. In the kitchen he reads Spinoza, and as he knots Bertie's tie, he quotes French epigrams. Like Holmes, he also has a more practical kind of knowledge. His mixture to cure hangovers will also relieve chronic dyspepsia. He has stored away, not in Holmesian scrapbooks, but in his amazing brain, details of the private lives of the people whom Bertie encounters in his adventures. He is decorous, even stuffy, but quite without scruple. To extricate Bertie from his plights, he steals, lies, bribes, blackmails, and uses violence. At least once he knocks out a constable with a blackjack.

Some people say that Bertie is too dependent on Jeeves, and

Aunt Agatha has even referred to Jeeves as Bertie's keeper. But Bertie's attitude is, why not? A week after Jeeves comes to him, he gives up all pretense of running his own life. Jeeves arrives when Bertie is in a very bad state, suffering the consequences of a drinking bout and trying to read a book about ethical theory touted to him by Florence Craye. At the time, Bertie is engaged to Florence, and she has asked him, as proof of his love, to confiscate the manuscript of the memoirs that one of Bertie's uncles is writing. These memoirs implicate Florence's father in a number of racy episodes. After Bertie snatches the manuscript, however, Jeeves mails it to the publisher, for he disapproves of the engagement, and besides, he knows that people actually like to have their checkered pasts written about.

Florence is furious and breaks the engagement; Bertie, in turn, is furious with Jeeves. Next day, however, he reflects that Florence, though beautiful, is domineering. Furthermore, he has been trying to read the second chapter of the book on ethics, and it is getting worse. In gratitude, he tells Jeeves that he may give away a suit over which they have had a disagreement (the pattern was attractive to Bertie, but Jeeves perceived that it was atrocious). Jeeves cooly replies that he has already given it to the under-gardener. Thus runs the plot of many a Bertie and Jeeves novel and short story; Jeeves fishes Bertie out of a difficulty, and Bertie sacrifices an abominable article of clothing, a mustache, a banjo, and so on.

Because of Jeeves's high-handedness, Bertie makes several attempts to get along without him. Once Jeeves threatens to leave if Bertie insists on practicing the banjolele, and Bertie insists. When Jeeves departs, Bertie is grieved but resolute: ". . . though I did not care to think of what existence would be like without Jeeves, I had no thought of weakening. As I turned the corner into Piccadilly, I was a thing of fire and chilled steel." [12] In a lonely hotel, however, Bertie moves about the room quietly, as though there were a death in the family. Later, trying to knot his own white tie, he understands the tears of things from another aspect. When at last Bertie meets Jeeves's terms, the reconciliation is like that between a man and his estranged wife. Indeed, Bertie says that it reminds him of such a situation in a novel. Bertie suffers even when Jeeves goes on his annual vacation to Herne Bay for the shrimp fishing. "A solemn moment," he says of their leave-taking, "taxing our self-control to the utmost." [13]

Bertie's role in the anomalous relation between master and servant is not so bad as it may sound. Jeeves would not take nonsense from any employer, whatever his stature (when he comes to Bertie, he has just resigned from the service of Lord Worplesdon, who likes to dine in dress trousers, flannel shirt, and shooting coat). Firm as he is, Jeeves always treats Bertie with every mark of respect. In fact, he indulges Bertie in all of the externals of the seigneur, so that Bertie can speak of Jeeves ushering guests "into the presence," or of "receiving" after he has drunk his tea in the morning. Thus Bertie has some right to talk of Jeeves's feudal spirit, a spirit which is illuminated by contrast when another valet, Brinkley, fills in briefly for Jeeves. Brinkley gets drunk and overstays his evening off. Returning at last, he thinks that Bertie, whose face (by the requirement of the plot) is covered with burnt cork, is the devil. He therefore chases Bertie with a carving knife. Even when sober Brinkley is bad enough, for he is a socialist type who believes that there should be no masters and no servants in the first place.

Finally, Bertie has a great admiration for Jeeves's intellect, which he recognizes, with touching candor, to be immeasurably superior to his own. "We must think, sir," Jeeves says in *Carry On, Jeeves* (1925). "You do it," Bertie replies. "I don't have the equipment." [14] Bertie reveres Jeeves's brain in itself, not merely as an instrument for getting him out of scrapes. Once Jeeves suggests a scheme which is as good as usual but which at the moment seems insane to Bertie, and Bertie is less concerned with what may happen to himself than with the tragic possibility that "that superb brain has come unstuck." [15]

Bertie is one of literature's idiots, but he is one of the most likable ones. However absurd he sounds when he speaks of his family's coming over with the Conqueror, of the chivalry of the Woosters, and the rest of it, he is in fact a very chivalrous fellow. Silly as he sounds when he speaks of the code of the Woosters, he lives by a code, all right, even if it is that of the schoolboy. When Bingo Little asks Bertie to steal and destroy a cylinder on which Mrs.

Little has dictated a revoltingly sentimental article on Bingo as a husband, he appeals to the fact that he and Bertie were at school together.

> "At school, Bertie, the dear old school."
> "I don't care. I will not—"
> "Bertie!"
> "I will not—"
> "Bertie!"
> "No!"
> "Bertie!"
> "Oh, all right." [16]

Bertie has at least enough sense to know that he is bargaining for trouble, but he cannot refuse.

Bertie's virtues also include gratitude and magnanimity. In *Jeeves in the Offing* (1960) Uncle Tom is arranging a business transaction with the American tycoon Homer Cream at the same time that Sir Roderick Glossop has been called in to check on the sanity of Cream's son Wilbert. Jeeves suggests that Sir Roderick say that he was called in to observe Bertie, so that Cream will not be offended and the transaction will go through. Though the plan means that Bertie will be branded as both a thief and a maniac, he agrees to it. For he remembers that when he was suffering under the rule of Upjohn at Malvern House, Uncle Tom sent him postal orders for as much as ten shillings. Jeeves tries to convince Bertie that the publicity will be confined to the guests at Brinkley Court, but Bertie knows better. The Creams will tell the story all over the United States, and he will be embarrassed no end on his next visit there.

Bertie is as ready to forgive old enemies as he is to do favors for old friends. At the conclusion of *The Code of the Woosters* Bertie has the magistrate Sir Watkyn Bassett in his power and dictates terms to him, but when the broken Bassett inquires whether there is brandy on the table and whether he may have some, Bertie says, "Jeeves, a snootful for Sir Watkyn." Then to the reader Bertie says, "He drained the beaker gratefully and tottered out. Probably quite a nice chap if you knew him." [17]

[114]

III *Other Comedians and Stereotypes*

There are three major comic characters of a greater age than
Bertie: Lords Emsworth, Marshmoreton, and Ickenham (Uncle
Fred). Lord Emsworth is an absentminded and inept gaffer who
can scarcely find his way to a table at the Senior Conservative
Club, even when he has his glasses on (more often they are hang-
ing down his back on their ribbon). Lord Emsworth drinks, but
only weak highballs, which are probably as much as his brain can
withstand. He would like to be left in peace to follow his hobbies
of raising prize pigs and pumpkins, but other residents of Blandings Castle frustrate him. If he allows his son Freddie to go up to
London, Freddie will get into some dreadful mess, but if he compels Freddie to stay at Blandings, he will be driven out of his
mind, such as it is. His sister Lady Constance is forever at him to
receive artists and poets or to work on a history of the family. (In
the time that he is supposed to have been writing it, more history has happened than Emsworth has written.) Then there is
Emsworth's secretary, Rupert Baxter, a combination of Pooh-Bah,
Nosey Parker, and the voice of conscience. Baxter is in and out of
his job in various novels and short stories—out because his virtues
are oppressive, and in because Blandings must have at least a little discipline. Baxter's very glasses, which he never loses, gleam
with efficiency, pierce through the consciences of the guilty, and
say to the consciences of the innocent, "Here is an efficient
young man in spectacles." [18]

Lord Marshmoreton is simply Lord Emsworth under another
name. Wodehouse gives him different obsessions (gardening in
corduroy trousers, squirting whale oil on insects), but the differences are insignificant, and the resemblances are marked: a family
history to write, a sister as chatelaine, a blockhead of a son.

Lord Ickenham (Uncle Fred), however, does not resemble
Lords Emsworth and Marshmoreton, nor does he resemble other
uncles in Wodehouse or elsewhere. More than sixty years old, he
says that he feels twenty-two, but he frequently cavorts on a level
below that of the twenties. He is still capable of regressing to the
age of the schoolboy and taking up with delight such old weapons as the slingshot and the peashooter. In more advanced moods,
he resembles Wodehouse's young men. Like Ukridge, he puts a

fundamental faith in the use of false names, and like dozens of the young heroes, he practices the art of impersonation, differing from them only in the boldness and variety of his masquerades. In his time, he has assumed such risky identities as those of Sir Roderick Glossop, the famous explorer Major Brabazon-Plank, and Inspector Jarvis of Scotland Yard, together with those of less notable figures and of persons whom he makes up on the spur of the moment.

Like Bingo Little, Uncle Fred has a wife who, knowing his character well, seldom permits him to carry large sums of money on him. Like Bertie Wooster, he has a poor opinion of magistrates, who (he has always found) impose fines when reprimands would be sufficient. Like Psmith, he is a nonstop talker and so constituted that the exercise of stirring up the people around him is vital to his well-being. In a rather alarming way, he also scatters sweetness and light and takes special satisfaction in befriending young lovers.

Uncle Fred is the presiding genius, if not the hero, of three novels, but the short story called "Uncle Fred Flits By" (1922) is a paradigm of his activities. On a visit to London, he drags his nephew Pongo on a pilgrimage to a suburb which once was the estate of their ancestors. (Here, Uncle Fred remembers sentimentally as he gazes about him, here must be the spot from which I shot the gardener in the pants with bow and arrow.) Caught in a sudden shower, they take refuge on the porch of one of the semidetached villas, but the rain still whips in upon them. Uncle Fred then rings the bell and informs the servant that he is the veterinarian, come to clip the parrot's claws (he has seen the bird through the window), and that Pongo is his assistant and gives the anesthetic. The servant, convinced, departs for her day off.

A young man named Robinson now calls, asking for the owner of the villa, Mr. Roddis, whereupon Uncle Fred says that he is Roddis and that Pongo is his son Douglas. Robinson explains that he is to meet his girl Julia, and soon the girl arrives with her parents, the Parkers. Mrs. Parker is the sister-in-law of Roddis, but because of a family quarrel, they have never met. Therefore, Uncle Fred continues to play Roddis, but he switches Pongo to the part of veterinarian, since the Parkers presumably know that Roddis does not have a son. Mrs. Parker says that Robinson is not worthy of her daughter, since he comes from a lower class. At this, Uncle Fred proceeds to draw some horrendous imaginary portraits of usurers, embezzlers, and drug-runners in the Parker family. He also gives Robinson a hundred pounds that Lady Ickenham has unwisely given him to pay a bill, so that the young man may purchase a small shop. (When Lady Ickenham asks him what became of the money, he will tell her that he gave it to Pongo, who needed it to buy back letters he had written to a Spanish demimondaine.)

Uncle Fred and Pongo leave the villa, but the Parkers, in a kind of empty assertion of will, remain to drink tea. While uncle and nephew are standing in the street outside the villa, the real Mr. Roddis appears; Uncle Fred introduces himself as J. G. Bulstrode and Pongo as Percy Frensham, an importer of lard and butter. In a last flourish, he adds that he observed two suspicious persons enter the villa. Having seen through the window that the Parkers are not only drinking his tea but presuming to open a jar of his raspberry jam, Roddis dashes off to fetch the police.

In the eighty-odd books there is a large supply of assorted comic stereotypes. There is no valet of importance besides Jeeves, but there are several butlers, all of them drawn pretty much from the same model, whether their names are Beach, Keggs, or something else. They are both regal and somewhat absurd. Though formidable, they are human, and as the boy Wodehouse once enjoyed teas in the servants' quarters presided over by the butler, Bertie Wooster has drunk many a glass of port in the pantry of Seppings, the butler at Aunt Dahlia's Brinkley Court.

Both the novels and the short stories are well populated by clergymen who, whether they are young or old, curates or bishops, incline to be militant, though not necessarily about religion. Augustine Mulliner, curate to the Reverend Stanley Brandon, is frequently afraid that his vicar will strike him. For example, in a slight difference of opinion over the arrangements for the Harvest Festival, "he thought for a moment that the vicar was going to drop him with a right hook to the chin." [19] Brandon is as belligerent with superiors as with subordinates, and he does not propose to be ordered about by Boko Bickerton, formerly his schoolmate and now his bishop. Because he once hit Boko in the eye for pouring ink on his collar, he does not have much respect for his spiritual authority. The bishop himself is no less aggressive, though he is grateful to Augustine for stopping him from attacking Brandon. "My fist was clenched, and I was just hauling off for the swing when you checked me." [20]

The secular arm comes off worse than the church. Most constables, bobbies, and detectives are Gilbert and Sullivan policemen put through the misadventures of Keystone Cops. In *The Mating Season* the village constable is also the village atheist and delights in baiting the vicar, popping out of side streets to make wisecracks about Jonah and to demand where Cain got his wife. It is this Constable Dobbs whom Jeeves blackjacks. Upon recovering consciousness, Dobbs thinks that he has been struck by a thunderbolt, and he forthwith gives up atheism.

The comic novels also include a miscellany of other stereotypes. Explorers have wiry frames, strong jaws, and keen eyes, and they are constantly reminded by the events in the story of similar events in places like the Federated Malay States. Crooks, who are sinister in the earliest novels, soon become, once and for all, innocuous and absurd. When they lose their female accomplices, they are reduced from one stratum of crime to another, for instance from safe-cracking to sticking up people in the streets. Lady novelists always write trash like *Only a Factory Girl* and *'Twas Once in May*. Barmaids are bright, amiable, and confidential, whereas teashop waitresses are depressed and depressing. And so it is with a great gallery of types from secretaries in the Foreign Office to boys who clean the knives and boots.

Wodehouse's years in the United States have provided him with a number of stock characters. Bertie Wooster believes that all American men fall into two main classes, the first of which is the friendly. The friendly man is stout, wears horn-rimmed glasses, chews gum incessantly with a perfect set of false teeth, dresses like a college student, and calls for fudge and waffles in all countries of the world. Sometimes his amiability modulates into rowdiness. Mr. Gedge, for instance, drinks too much, goes through several moods from exuberance (" 'Ee-yah! Ee-yah! Ee-yah!' he whooped, jumping rapidly up and down" [21]) to sentimentality to belligerence, and finally passes out with his face in a dish of ice cream. This type plays Jiggs to his wife's Maggie. Mrs. Gedge informs her husband that she is going to get him appointed ambassador to France whether he likes it or not. *That* will show her previous husband's sister, who sneered that she had remarried beneath her. Mrs. Steptoe vows that she will smarten up her husband Howard if it is the last thing she does.

Bertie says that the other type of American runs to cold stares and square jaws. He must have in mind particularly the sub-class of the financier, who is tough, determined, and accustomed to having his way. Having learned that it took his doctor many years to assemble a collection of scarabs, J. Preston Peters bets the doctor that he can make an equivalent collection in six months. Told that you cannot bribe the British police, J. Washburn Stoker is incredulous. What American businessmen do when they are not engaged in business, Bertie has not yet discovered; but he surmises that they go into a kind of coma, emerging from it the following day when it is time to do business again.

For this single-minded pursuit, and perhaps for too many rich dinners and large cigars, financiers pay with dyspepsia. From J. Preston Peters (whose valet reads him to sleep with extracts from a cookbook) in *Something Fresh* to the most recent example, there is probably not a single eupeptic financier. George Stoker, the father of J. Washburn Stoker, is said to have suffered from another kind of illness. "This George," says Bertie, "was a man who, after a lifetime of doing down the widow and orphan, had begun to feel the strain a bit. His conversation was odd, and he had a tendency to walk on his hands." [22] The financier also has difficulties with his wives and his ex-wives. Elmer Chinnery, the fish glue king, pays alimony to a squad of wives, and so does Vincent Jopp. The otherwise indomitable Jopp nearly goes the way of George Stoker when several of his ex-wives follow him about the golf course, one of them nagging him about his health, another criticizing the look of his legs in plus fours, still another talking baby talk to her Pekinese.

IV *Farce and Other Comic Forms*

Wodehouse is at his best as a writer of farce, by which I do not mean mere slapstick, though there is plenty of that in Wodehouse. If there is a vast deal of violence, there is no serious injury. Punches are thrown, but not so many as are threatened, and, generally speaking, the weapons used are the kind that make the most commotion and do the least harm. When eggs and bottles of champagne are flung through windows, it is the eggs that strike people. Vases, which are likely to miss the victim and splatter all over the place, are more common than blackjacks, which are efficient and silent. Various other kinds of assault without deadly weapons are common. For example, three young nincompoops bring back the seasickness of a dowager on the pier by smoking cigars at her, waving their arms to indicate the pitching of the ship, theorizing about the causes of seasickness (is the main reason, after all, the smell of the engine grease?), and offering her food. But more common than this sort of thing is mere schoolboy prankishness: stealing people's clothes while they are swimming, snatching their hats from neighboring cabs, puncturing their hot water bottles (a classic maneuver on country-house terrain).

Wodehouse's adaptation of certain devices of melodrama is of equal importance. The mechanics of melodrama—the sudden entrances and exits, disguises, secrets, discoveries, contretemps, coincidences—translate, in fact, very easily into farce. In the following speech, Bertie Wooster suggests both the connection between the two forms of literature and Wodehouse's long familiarity with melodrama: ". . . I am a man of wide reading. Starting in early boyhood, long before they were called novels of suspense, I've read more mystery stories than you could shake a stick at, and they have taught me something—viz. that anybody with something to hide invariably puts it on top of the cupboard, or, if you prefer it, the armoire. This is what happened in *Murder at Mistleigh Manor, Three Dead on Tuesday, Excuse My Gat, Guess Who,* and a dozen other standard works." [23]

In the comic novels Wodehouse makes more use of the crimes of melodramatic literature than he makes in the romantic novels. The incidence of larceny is particularly high. Aunt Dahlia, for example, is an ardent practitioner and advocate of larcenous methods of getting what she wants, though she does not always regard them as such. By her system of casuistry, if a collector of silver, like her husband Tom, pinches something from another collector, he is not really stealing. People less raffish than Aunt Dahlia likewise incline to or actually engage in theft, together with other assorted crimes. Sir Watkyn Bassett, who, as a retired magistrate and still justice of the peace, should set a good example, is:

constantly trying to steal Aunt Dahlia's cook. Among the kidnappers is J. Washburn Stoker, who locks Bertie Wooster in a stateroom on a yacht to force him to marry Pauline. A supposedly respectable American woman says that if Monty Bodkin is, as he appears to be, a detective, he is still bribable like anyone else. And women young and old, American and British, are instinctive smugglers through the customs, on the theory that the government has too much money already and would only spend it if it got more.

Not the least popular of crimes are blackmail and extortion. Aunt Dahlia speaks for multitudes, exclaiming at a time when all seems lost, "Good old blackmail! You can't beat it. I've always said so, and I always shall." [24] Aunt Dahlia threatens Bertie with an end to invitations to dine unless he steals things for her. Stiffy Byng threatens to turn Madeline Bassett loose on him. To force Aubrey Upjohn to drop a libel suit against Bertie's friend Kipper Herring, Jeeves devises a plan to steal and hold a manuscript without which Upjohn cannot make an important speech. Sir Waykyn will press charges against Bertie unless Uncle Tom turns the chef, Anatole, over to him. In one novel there is an instance of reciprocal blackmail. Mr. Gedge is blackmailing Senator Opal at the same time that Packy Franklyn (on behalf of Senator Opal) is blackmailing Mrs. Gedge.

The finest of theaters for Wodehouse's comedy is the country house. A place like Chuffnell Regis, with its hundred and fifty rooms and miles upon miles of rolling parkland may be a white elephant to the owner, but it is priceless to the farceur. On the grounds there are ponds, lakes, and even moats to push people into; there are boathouses, stables, and potting sheds to lock them in. Around the house there are shrubs to duck into and trees to climb when pursued. Inside, there are so many bedrooms that guests can get lost and enter the wrong one by mistake, or hide in one which they think is empty but which turns out to be occupied.

Among other stage properties, there are countless small objects to be thrown about and broken or smashed by accident. Of these, Wodehouse's favorite is a statuette of the Infant Samuel in prayer. (In Wodehouse, even French hotels are furnished with copies of this work; a golfing character breaks one while practicing chip shots in his room at the Hotel Superb.) In places like Totleigh Towers and Brinkley Court these are shattered as if they were so many clay pigeons. Also there are plenty of small tables, covered with china ornaments or other objects large and small. At Blandings, one table holds, together with other things, a vase, a jar of potpourri, an Indian sandalwood box, and a large photograph of Lord Emsworth's eldest son, Lord Bosham.

But large and complicated objects are not lacking either. In one encounter, extraordinary even by the standards of Totleigh Towers, Bertie Wooster collides in the darkness with a grandfather clock. "Glass crashed, pulleys and things parted from their moorings." [25] Bertie knocks the clock flat, but it also floors him. When, after a complicated lot of prowling, spying, and rushing about has taken place in the dark, the lights go on in Blandings Castle, some startling tableaux are revealed. In one of them, the stairs are full of half-dressed people, and the hall is littered with overturned tables and broken china. The dinner gong has a dent in it from the shot that Lord Emsworth has fired at the burglars whom he suspected to be in the Castle. At the foot of the stairs, Baxter lies unconscious. He is clad in an overcoat and tennis shoes, and his face is pillowed on some bread, cold tongue, a bottle of wine, and a corkscrew.

Both by day and by night there are terrible combats in country houses. In *The Code of the Woosters,* two small men, Bertie and Gussie Fink-Nottle, do battle with one large one, Roderick Spode. Gussie smashes an oil painting over Spode's head, and Bertie follows by enveloping Spode in a sheet. Spode reaches out a hand, but he withdraws it when Bertie applies a lighted cigarette. Then Bertie turns to flee and collides with Aunt Dahlia, who is entering the room at her top speed. They roll around on the floor in confusion at the same time that Spode, still wrapped in his sheet, is thrashing about. Reaching out again, Spode grasps Aunt Dahlia by the ankle. "And now," she cries, "the gentleman in the burnous has started tickling my ankle—a thing that hasn't happened to me since the York and Ainsty Hunt Ball of the year nineteen-twenty-one." [26]

Country houses also offer unusual opportunities for practical jokes. In this regard, Bertie Wooster's criticism of the small boy Seabury shows the eye of a connoisseur. Seabury, says Bertie, with an entire country house lying before him, makes a soot-and-water booby trap on the top of a door, a device which he could have rigged up in a simple suburban villa. Bertie is still more critical of Seabury's failure to make the proper use of the medium on another occasion, when Seabury plans a butter-slide for Sir Roderick Glossop. "I was disgusted. Goodness knows that any outrage perpetrated on the person of a bloke like Sir Roderick Glossop touches a ready chord in Bertram Wooster's bosom, but a butter-slide. . . . the lowest depths as you might say. The merest A B C of the booby-trapping art. There isn't a fellow at the Drones who would sink to such a thing." [27]

Furthermore, there are a great many things to steal in country houses. Always, there is silver; always, there are paintings. Besides such standard items of the inventory, there may be collections of one sort or another. At Blandings there once was a large collection room teeming with Lord Emsworth's scarabs. At Brinkley Court, Uncle Tom's silver collection is still intact, unless a rival happens to have pinched the most precious piece in it, the cow creamer. The occasions for masquerades and mistaken identities are also usefully numerous. Because so many guests, unknown by sight to their fellow guests, and sometimes to their host, are arriving and departing, impersonations can take place right and left. Because extra servants are needed on special occasions, people can breach the castle walls as valets and cooks. Once even the forbidding Sir Roderick Glossop poses as a butler, adopting (of all possible aliases) the name Swordfish, and simpering modestly when complimented on the skill with which he plays his role.

But there is more to Wodehouse's comedy than people clouting each other, racing in and out of rooms, and wearing false mustaches or false names. The example of Wilde, as Eric Bentley has remarked, demonstrates that there is no contradiction between farce and verbal felicity.[28] Wodehouse, indeed, sometimes says things that are reminiscent of Wilde. Of a woman who collects dry seaweed and pastes it in scrapbooks, a nephew says that it looks as if some aunts live entirely for pleasure. But by the mention of Wilde, I do not mean to suggest that Wodehouse's language is always subtle. Frequently it is very broad and obvious, beginning with the names of his characters: Puffy Benger, Galahad Threepwood, Hermione Brimble, Lord Blicester ("old blister" is a favorite expression of Wodehouse's young men). Wodehouse also has the habit of hyperbole. When a single constable appears in Deverill Hall, Bertie Wooster remarks that the place is filling up with rozzers, and this is how Esmond Haddock alludes to Bertie's pinching one or two policemen's helmets: "Whenever Wooster has a spare moment, he goes about London persecuting unfortunate policemen, assaulting them, hampering them in their duties, making their lives a hell on earth." [29] And Wodehouse is not above writing such dumb-broad dialogue as the following:

"Suppose, for instance, that he could be made to believe that you were . . . a dypsomaniac."
She shook her head. "He knows that already."
"What!"
"Yes; I told him I sometimes walk in my sleep."
"I mean a secret drinker."
"Nothing will induce me to pretend to be a secret drinker."
"Then a drug fiend?" I suggested hopefully.
"I hate medicine." [30]

But such instances are extremes. Actually, verbal nuances are a major concern of Wodehouse's, as Bertie Wooster's address to the reader near the end of *The Mating Season* indicates. "In dishing up this narrative for family consumption, it has been my constant aim throughout to get the right word in the right place and avoid fobbing the customers off with something weak and inexpressive when they have the right to expect the telling phrase. It means a bit of extra work, but one has one's code. . . . We will therefore expunge that 'came' at the conclusion of the previous spasm and substitute 'curvetted.'" [31] (Esmond Haddock has just entered, euphoric because he has read the riot act to his five aunts.) The names that Wodehouse gives his characters do not lack respectable precedent. Wilde bestows upon his people such names as Miss Prism and the Reverend Mr. Chasuble, and the best writers of Restoration comedy provide such examples as Sir Tunbelly Clumsy, Syringe (for a doctor), Pinchwife, and Sir Fopling Flutter. As for the hyperbole, it is hyperbole with a flair, an exaggeration that is not merely mathematical, but poetic.

The more complex resources of Wodehouse's verbal comedy include his immense and various vocabulary, his inexhaustible stock of quotations and allusions, his profusion of bright new figures of speech, and his deliberately mad mixtures of both old and new metaphors. Wodehouse has at easy command the terminologies of science and theology on the one hand (in the Anglers' Rest, the patrons discuss supralapsarianism over their evening drinks), and the slang of more than one century on the other. The literary allusions and quotations run not only down the ages from the Greeks to the present, but also down the scale from Shakespeare to minor writers like Thomas Hood and Felicia Hemans.

The principle on which Wodehouse exploits this treasure house of masterpieces and trash is a controlled disparity. Mrs. Cream's thrillers, for instance, fill her readers with pity and terror; Bertie and Jeeves will meet at Philippi; moans are wrenched from the lips of silly young men as though from souls in agony. Working on his own, Wodehouse describes a miser, who in a forgetful moment has loaned ten pounds, as writhing like an electric fan; a beautiful girl as looking like Helen of Troy after a good facial; a trouble-making girl as having the disposition of a ticking bomb. In the scrambling of the familiar, cauliflower ears hide hearts of gold, and Bertie doubts that Lady Wickham would telephone him with a ten-foot pole.

Wodehouse is at the top of his form with Bertie Wooster, and one of the things that makes the Wooster stories and novels so good is that Bertie narrates them. Bertie is very ignorant and, at the same time, enormously learned. For example, he believes that Queen Elizabeth and Boadicea were contemporaries, but he is something of an expert on scriptural knowledge (at school he won a prize in this area, as he often reminds his friends and the reader). On one occasion he will miss an obvious Shakespearean tag of Jeeves's, but on another he will quote Shakespeare as well as Jeeves. He is slangy and informal in his speech, yet he is also aware of grammatical precision and propriety, and conscious of levels of diction. Thus, he reports Aunt Dahlia in a rage at Aubrey Upjohn:

"Oh?" she said, "So you have decided to revise my guest list for me? You have the nerve, the—the—"
I saw she needed helping out.
"Audacity," I said, throwing her the line.

"The audacity to dictate to me who I shall have in my house."

It should have been "whom," but I let it go.

"You have the—"

"Crust."

"—the immortal rind," she amended, and I had to admit it was stronger, "to tell me whom"—she got it right that time—"I may entertain at Brinkley Court and who"—wrong again—"I may not." [32]

Of Sir Roderick Glossop, Bertie says, "Having [chuckled], he blessed his soul, which was his way of saying 'Gorblimey.'" [33] Bertie has to have Jeeves finish his sentences for him, and even his clichés. He tells Jeeves that he is in sore somethings or is on the horns of something, and Jeeves has to supply "straits" or "dilemma." More often, however, Bertie is fluency itself.

Even at its most fluent, Bertie's speech obeys Wodehouse's law of controlled incongruity. It is a marvelous hodgepodge in which rare and extravagant words are followed by standard English, and standard English expressions are followed by colloquial and trite ones. It is, above all, a speech of unconscious ironies. "Those who know Bertram Wooster best," says Bertie, "are aware that he is a man of sudden, strong enthusiasms, and that, when in the grip of one of these, he becomes a machine—tense, absorbed, single-minded. It was so in the matter of this banjolele-playing of mine." [34] Similarly, Bertie takes a cigarette or a piece of cake in a marked manner. Kipper Herring asks him what he is grinning about, and Bertie tells the reader that he was, in fact, smiling subtly but that he let it go. When Stiffy Byng becomes angry, because he will not undertake one of her mad schemes, and tells him that he is a pig, he replies that she may be right, but that he is a shrewd, level-headed sort of pig.

Through all of his writing Wodehouse scatters pieces of parody, and in the short stories he often writes sustained parodies, especially of the love story and the success story. In three books of short stories (*Meet Mr. Mulliner*, 1927; *Mr. Mulliner Speaking*, 1929; *Mulliner Nights*, 1933), the raconteur of the Anglers' Rest entertains the patrons of the bar-parlor with the adventures of his countless nephews. The clergyman Augustine Mulliner, for example, wins not only his girl but also preferment by throwing rocks at a dog and hitting him smartly in the ribs with one. For this dog once chased Augustine's bishop up a tree, and also got his

vicar by the ankle while he was walking along the river compos-
ing a sermon. A lay Mulliner, a drinker, gambler, and general gay
blade, pretends to be a strait-laced and pious fellow because the
girl he loves comes from a clerical family; but she concludes that
he is the dullest man on earth and rejects him. Only when he is
blamed for the drunken brawling of someone else, does she decide that he is interesting enough to marry after all.

Wodehouse frequently parodies the sentimental novel and
play à la Sir James Matthew Barrie. James Rodman, a writer of
detective stories, inherits Honeysuckle Cottage from his aunt, on
the condition that he live in it for six months of the year. When he
tries to write in the wretched cottage, he finds that the influence
of his aunt—and the soppy novels that she wrote—has filtered
into his tough stories, making them soppy too, populating them
with tender heroes and coy heroines. Next he finds himself living such a story when a girl, struck by a car, recuperates in the
cottage. This story is complete with kindly old doctor, apple-
cheeked housekeeper, and guardian of the girl who is in love with
her. The latter is an old soldier, bravely giving the girl up, ma-
neuvering to force James to propose, though his keen old blue
eyes are full of pain. From all of this James escapes to London
with his dog. Less frequently Wodehouse parodies the melodrama
and the spy story. Clarence Mulliner is visited by a man who
wears a black velvet mask and tells him: "No doubt you are
aware, Mr. Mulliner, that for some time this country and a certain
rival Power have been competing for the friendship and alliance
of a certain other Power?" [35]

In two volumes of stories about golf, Wodehouse combines
parody with the comedy of humors, giving the latter a more thorough workout than it has got since Thomas Shadwell. In these
stories the golf course is Wodehouse's image of the world, his fair
field of folk and his ship of fools, as Bertie Wooster might say.
Golf is not only a sport, but also an occupation and a religion; the
course is the poser of ethical problems and the tester of character.

The stories are narrated by the Oldest Member, who is, in effect, Mr. Mulliner, transferred from the public house to the club
house. A wise-old-man figure (Wodehouse refers to him as "the
Sage"), he sits near the eighteenth green and looks over the fairways and the rough as though over the great globe itself. Stocked

with the observations of a lifetime, he acts as father-confessor and advisor to the members of the club, regarding them with some detachment, but also with some pity for their youth. His favorite philosopher is Marcus Aurelius, whom he recommends in all difficulties, and he believes that Marcus Aurelius was a golfer himself, a very incompetent one who went around in a hundred and twenty on a good day. ("Nothing happens to anybody which he is not fitted to bear," he thinks, must have come to the Emperor after he had sliced two or three new balls into a woods, and must have been noted down on the back of his score card.)

Wodehouse's inventiveness enables him to write about monomaniacs without being monotonous. The characters are said to have jobs in brokers' offices and publishing houses, but they have time to play thirty-six holes every day. When day is done, they read and dream of golf. In their homes they have studies, but apparently the only books on the shelves are copies of *The Meditations of Marcus Antoninus* and extensive collections of golf manuals written by the champions of the game since its beginnings. One character brings surrealism into the world of golf, dreaming that a cow has appeared to him and earnestly advised him to change his grip from the interlocking to the two-V.

As Wodehouse turns a golf course into the world, one of his players turns the world into a golf course. Mortimer Sturgis, touring Italy on his honeymoon, regards the entire country, natural and man-made alike, as nothing more than a series of long and short holes, hazards, and traps. The Temple of Vespasian, he considers, would be a terrible place to be bunkered behind. He wonders whether Abe Mitchell could carry the Colosseum with anything less than a full brassie. As for the view over the Tuscan Hills from the Torre Rosa, Fiesole, it looks to him like an extremely bad stretch of rough. The problems of the characters are not altogether confined to golf. For instance, there are enough frustrated lovers in the stories to make up a tournament. But when lovers are reconciled or soul-mate has found soul-mate, golf has the last word. "He folded her in his arms," runs the concluding sentence of one of the stories, "using the interlocking grip." [36]

CHAPTER 6

The Wodehouse World

I   From Reality to Fantasy

THE world of Wodehouse's novels and short stories *exists*, like other successful literary worlds, but it is unreal in a way that some such worlds are not. I do not mean merely that the plots (though ingenious) are preposterous and the characters grotesque, for the same could be said of much of the work of Evelyn Waugh. Yet, however extravagant the happenings, however caricatured the people, Waugh's world is nonetheless a recognizable reflection of the real one. Wodehouse's is not, and usually it is not intended to be.

In a few of the earliest novels, however, and in spots of a few later ones, Wodehouse endeavored to write about real men and women in a real world. As any young writer might, he did exercises in literary description—storms at sea and landscapes of various sorts under various conditions, some of them extremely bleak. In *Jill the Reckless* there is a grim picture of an abortive real estate development on Long Island in winter, an ugly and barren area with stubbled fields surrounding the few houses and a railway station. (The geography of the later books omits all such landscapes and atmospheres, and in the area around Blandings Castle the weather is even better than it is in T. H. White's Camelot.)

In *Jill the Reckless*, Wodehouse even tried to get down to the bedrock reality of economic facts. Walking along the Thames Embankment, Jill reflects on the jobless men who will sleep there later in the night, and soon afterwards she is looking for work herself. In *Something Fresh*, the first volume in the comic cycle of Blandings Castle, Wodehouse describes the demoralizing effects of a fruitless search for work. "It is the saddest spectacle in the world, that of the crowd collected by a 'Wanted' advertisement. They are so palpably not wanted by anyone for any purpose whatever; yet every time they gather together with a sort of hopeful hopelessness."[1] In *The Coming of Bill* (1920) Wodehouse praises the courage of the little nursery maid who carries on after her father has lost his job, her younger brothers have become ill, and the life of the family has become one disaster after another.

Wodehouse always sees the figure of the financier bestriding the economic world like a colossus, but the financier of the early books looks very different from the one of the later books. He is unreal, a cliché of melodrama, but Wodehouse intends him to be genuine. Old J. B., the father of Ruth Bannister, cares for nothing but money and power. He has no love for family, affection for friends, or interest in culture (musicians and writers are tolerable only because they entertain him for a moment now and then). In *The Prince and Betty* (1912) there is a greater scoundrel of a financier, Benjamin Scobell, who buys up (among other things) the lovely Mediterranean island of Mervo to turn it into a profitable business. "He was a nasty little man," says Wodehouse, "to hold despotic sway over such a paradise: a goblin in fairyland. Somewhat below the middle height, he was lean of body and vulturine of face. He had a greedy mouth, a hooked nose, liquid green eyes, and a sallow complexion."[2] The financier is, indeed, so great a monster that even aunts become likable by contrast. Though Ruth Bannister's aunt Mrs. Porter is a dogmatist and a busybody, she is admirable in that she stands up to the tyrant Bannister. And Betty's aunt Mrs. Oakley earns high marks for keeping Scobell scared to death lest she cut him out of her will.

In the earliest novels Wodehouse also treats love, marriage, and family life as serious subjects. His explorations of the contradictions and complexities of love will surprise readers familiar with the later work only. For instance, he allows Betty to learn that she loves John but also hates him, admires him but also despises him. And he follows Ruth and Kirk Winfield beyond engagement to marriage, a failure of marriage, a drifting apart, and a final reconciliation. (In Ruth, Wodehouse also essays a portrait of the "new woman," one who knows about subjects like eugenics and discusses them openly, to the dismay of her brother, who thinks that nice girls have never so much as heard of them.)

As father, John Bannister is no Sir Anthony Absolute, all sound and futile fury, but a martinet who arranges his children's lives as

if they were portfolios of stocks, and finally, as in any melodrama, disowns his daughter when she marries without his approval. "His was a patriarchical mind, and he welcomed opportunities of exercising his authority over his children. It had always
been his policy to rule them masterfully, and he had often re-
sented the fact that his daughter was to a great extent outside his
immediate rule." [3] Even the uncle who holds the purse strings and
believes that nephews should work hard, is a serious character. In
The Prince and Betty, John's uncle hates John for the illogical reason that he hated John's father; provided with the shadow of a
justification, he gives John the money held in trust from his
mother, then throws him out of his office, out of his life.

Another comic stereotype of the later books, the wealthy
woman of many marriages, is the most thoroughly done of all the
serious studies in the early books. Though she is in some respects
a combination of Miss Havisham and Hetty Green, Mrs. Oakley did
not begin life as a rich girl. The daughter of an impoverished Vermont farmer, she was crushed when the rich boy whom she loved
deserted her to marry a rich woman. She left the farm and entered the business world (Wodehouse draws a portrait of another
kind of "new woman"), taught herself typing, shorthand, and
bookkeeping, and eventually married her employer. Upon his
death, she inherited a great fortune; married again, she was wid-
owed again and acquired a second fortune.

Mrs. Oakley's attitude to money, conditioned by her early life,
is curious and probably psychotic. She feels truly sorry for the poor,
raises money for charities, gives inspirational talks to working
girls, but cannot bring herself to give away a penny. Still resent-
ful about her girlhood romance, she lives in seclusion, waited
upon by one servant and surrounded by a huge collection of
clocks. The one dearest to her is not the most expensive, but one
that she loved in the Vermont farmhouse (a little man is pro-
jected from it and sounds the hours on a toy trumpet). To Betty,
who has fled from her father and her lover, the old woman gives a
bitter prescription distilled from her own experience: "I wanted
to kill my heart [lest it kill me]. And I killed it. There's only one
way. Work!" [4]

The main line of Wodehouse, however, even in the early work,
is a flight from reality. Perhaps he found it too painful to dwell on

the look of men out of work, and probably he came more and more to realize that serious fiction was not his métier. In any event, he turned away from gravity and grimness soon enough. The year before he published *The Coming of Bill*, the nearest thing to a conventional novel that he ever wrote, he published *My Man Jeeves* (1919). Midway in realistic sections of other novels, he suddenly shifts into fantasy. In *Jill the Reckless* he writes a documentary about chorus girls waiting for jobs in a new musical (a more elaborate equivalent of the passage on the men answering the want ad), but then he turns the documentary into a romantic adventure. Jill strides by the other girls, the office boy, and the switchboard girl into the office and gets a job, not because the casting director finds her qualified (she is not), but because the writer of the show instantly falls in love with her.

After making some brave stabs at realism in *The Prince and Betty*, Wodehouse provides a most improbable happy ending. Mrs. Oakley, who never gave anyone a nickel, gives Betty and John one hundred thousand dollars to buy a ranch. By the time of *The Luck of the Bodkins* (1935) any traffic with reality is a token affair. There are references to the Depression and the New Deal, but most people are worrying about the usual broken engagements, tyrannical wives, interfering aunts, and customs officials. The few characters who worry about getting jobs get them, all right, not by the laws of economics, but by the laws of farce.

Wodehouse's world is, in many ways, so much like that of the musical comedies in which he was involved, that the usual publisher's disclaimer that all of the characters are purely imaginary and have no resemblance to living people, is superfluous. Though beautiful, the girls are, in accord with some mysterious system of genetics, begotten by men and women who look like walruses and horses. The young men all fit neatly into one category or another of a casting office. At the end of the novels, couples are separated and paired off in a way consistent with the statutes of Gilbert and Sullivan, as amended by writers of twentieth-century musicals. Wodehouse is, of course, perfectly aware of what he is doing. At the end of *Uncle Dynamite*, Uncle Fred, who has done much to arrange the separating and the pairing, remarks, "It reminds one of the final spasm of a musical comedy." [5] Most older people are not like Uncle Fred, but like Lord Emsworth or Sir

Buckstone Abbott, not much interested in the world around them aside from a mania or two, willing to live and let live, too absent-minded to keep track of their hats and glasses, too stupid to solve the simplest crossword puzzle. Older women are only too much interested in the affairs of others, always on the *qui vive,* and re-solved to dominate. If they were not outmaneuvered from time to time, Wodehouse's world would be an absolute matriarchy.

The business and professional men who are presumably run-ning the world are, if anything, more fantastic than the other characters. In all businessmen there is a touch of the crook, though after the earliest novels the money that they steal is, as it were, counterfeit. Financiers are called buccaneers and pirates of the Spanish Main, but they are pirates out of a Christmas panto-mime. Though they have granite jaws, they are stooges to their wives, nieces, and physical-training instructors. As represented by Wodehouse's constables and magistrates, the law is in worse shape than business. Bertie Wooster says that if you show him a magistrate, he will show you a fathead and, given only Bertie's evidence, one would have to reach Bertie's conclusion. Policemen no longer practice brutality and graft, but go around saying, "Ho!" and, "Here, what's all this?" and getting their helmets pinched. Like Lord Emsworth, Constable Potter finds that his authority is nothing to his women. He cannot call his life his own, since half belongs to his sister, who wants him to stay on the force, and half belongs to his fiancée, who wants him to buy a pub with the money he has won on football pools.

Education, of course, is represented by the bizarre Aubrey Up-john. Boko Bickerton, the prelate with the boxer's instincts, is an example of the older churchman; and Harold Pinker, the former football player, is an example of the younger. Stiffy Byng's part in the following dialogue illustrates the affable irreverence with which the layman regards the church. Stiffy is asking her Uncle, Sir Watkyn, to bestow on her fiancé, Harold Pinker, a vicarage which is in his giving. In a good mood because he has just learned that Gussie Fink-Nottle is not going to be his son-in-law, Sir Watkyn readily agrees.

"Of course, of course, of course, of course," he said, carolling like one of Jeeves' larks on the wing. "I am sure that Harold will make an excellent vicar."

"The best," said Stiffy. "He's wasted as a curate. No scope. He's running under wraps. Unleash him as a vicar, and he'll be the talk of the established church. He's hot as a pistol."

"I have always had the highest opinion of Harold Pinker."

"I'm not surprised. All the nibs feel the same way. They know he's got what it takes. Very sound on doctrine, and can preach like a streak." [6]

Wodehouse nearly ignores politics and politicians altogether. In view of the accusations of Fascism brought against Wodehouse in World War II, it is ironical that the only full-length portrait of a political figure is a satirical one of a British Fascist in a novel published in 1938, *The Code of the Woosters*. Roderick Spode is the founder and head of an organization known officially as the Saviors of Britain and unofficially as the Black Shorts. Spode's ambition, provided that he does not get brained in one of the brawls that he and his followers provoke, is to become dictator of the United Kingdom. (By 1953, in *Stiff Upper Lip, Jeeves,* Spode has become Lord Sidcup and has apparently dropped Fascism, but he is still as obnoxious as anyone in the late novels.) The usually good-natured Bertie says to Spode, "The trouble with you, Spode, is that just because you have succeeded in inducing a handful of half-wits to disfigure the London scene by going about in black shorts, you think you're someone. You hear them shouting, 'Heil, Spode!' and you imagine that is the Voice of the People. That is where you make your bloomer. What the Voice of the People is saying is: 'Look at that frightful ass Spode swanking about in footer bags.'" [7] Spode is not only the loud-mouthed founder of the Black Shorts, but also the secret founder, proprietor, and designer of Eulalie Soeurs, a Bond Street shop for ladies' underclothing. Thus he is vulnerable to blackmail when Bertie learns his secret, and so he cannot dictate even to a few people at Totleigh Towers.

In Wodehouse, values are reversed so that, for example, certain ordinary, prosaic, and trivial experiences are terrifying. It is axiomatic that judging a bonnie baby contest is one of the most perilous enterprises in which a man can engage. Young fellows like Bingo Little are frankly scared to death of them, and even a dauntless explorer like Major Brabazon-Plank is frightened, for he still carries the scar of a stab wound inflicted by a disgruntled Peruvian mother after he awarded first prize to another woman's child.

On the other hand, dangerous and criminal activities become commonplace and, as it were, domesticated. Nobody, including Wodehouse, worries about distinctions between acts that have extenuating circumstances and acts that do not. Psmith steals the diamond necklace of Lady Constance and gives it to her husband Joe, so that he can pawn it and give the money to his daughter to buy a farm. If Lady Constance would permit Joe to give Phyllis the money directly, the stealing of the necklace would, of course, be unnecessary. Joe will present Lady Constance with another necklace, and he gave her the stolen one in the first place, so, in a sense, there is no theft. In most cases, however, no such elaborate rationale is involved. Somebody simply wants a jewel, a manuscript, or a portrait, and he or an agent forthwith sets out to steal it. Once (lest a critical letter tie him for life to Madeline Bassett) Bertie Wooster even intercepts His Majesty's mails. And the professional criminal is just as innocuous as the amateur; like the other occupations, crime becomes one more joke.

II *Victorian and Edwardian*

The Wodehouse world is removed from reality in that it is in part an earlier world, a period world, for Wodehouse, after all, comes out of an earlier time. In 1953, reading the letters that he wrote to William Townend, he reflects upon the thirty years that they cover and the people mentioned in them, many no longer alive. Among the dead are George Horace Lorimer, Marilyn Miller, George Grossmith, Jerome Kern, Flo Ziegfeld, and George Gershwin. But these people were mostly the friends of Wodehouse's middle years; his literary and theatrical ties reach as far back as the turn of the century. He was a member of the Beefsteak Club when Kipling was still a member, and he was a correspondent of Kipling. As a young man, he once dined with W. S. Gilbert, whom he incensed by laughing at a joke before Gilbert got to the point of it. As a boy, of course, he read the works of nineteenth-century writers as they appeared. In March of 1949 he is saddened that *Strand* is appearing for the last time, since he not only read the magazine in boyhood, but also wrote for it from 1905 on. And he published his first school novel three years before he placed anything in *Strand*.

Since Wodehouse wrote his first fourteen books in the reign of Edward VII, they are bound to date in many ways. In *Psmith in the City*, people ride in "taximeter cabs," and the cricket team of a local regiment arrives at the school Ilsworth in a "brake." In *Something Fresh* an auto takes guests from the railway station to Blandings Castle, but an uncovered cart, drawn by snorting horses, conveys the guests' servants. Chorus girls, who are not yet called chorus girls, but "the personnel of the ensemble," are statuesque creatures with hourglass figures who gaze dreamy-eyed at the audience and lean on long parasols.

Moreover, there are anachronisms in the later books right down to the present. Some of them, no doubt, are the results of habit, carelessness, or indifference. In 1938 a car is going very fast when it is traveling at fifty-five miles per hour. In 1948 automobiles still have running boards. In 1960 Bertie Wooster tells the reader that he is smoking the kind of cigarette that makes one nonchalant, a reference to a brand long off the market. ("Be nonchalant. Light a Murad," the advertising copy ran.) More often, however, the anachronisms are clearly deliberate. Wodehouse perpetrates some of them because they appeal to his sense of the absurd, because they have an antiquarian smack. For example, in a novel published in 1960, Bertie Wooster asks Bobbie Wickham what she supposes Upjohn intends to do in London, and she replies that he probably went to discover who wrote an article attacking him, so that he could horsewhip the fellow on the steps of his club. Wodehouse commits other anachronisms because they are part of his equipment as a professional novelist, because he has used them successfully for so many years. Thus he continues to write of village concerts at which baritones sing "The Yeoman's Wedding Song," of village fetes with bun-eating contests and egg-and-spoon races; thus he writes as though people wore pince-nez and men wore spats.

But the most important reason for the anachronisms is that Wodehouse is repelled by much of the modern world and is taking refuge from it. He is dismayed by the violence, crime, and obscenity that he finds reflected in art and literature, both popular and otherwise. "Those Southerners!" he says, after reading William Faulkner's *Sanctuary*.[8] He finds *The Naked and the Dead* an absorbing book, but an indication of the change that has come over the world of letters, since Mailer puts into a novel words that once were put only on lavatory walls. The current books that he enjoys are often those that get out of the twentieth century altogether, like *The Sword in the Stone* and *Mistress Masham's Repose*.

Chronological salients and retreats make the temporal boundaries of Wodehouse's own world somewhat irregular, but one might say that it is roughly limited on one side by the Diamond Jubilee of Queen Victoria and on the other by the introduction of the crossword puzzle. It is a world in which not only butlers but also boys who clean the knives and boots are taken for granted, in which golf is a game played by well-to-do people on private courses. At its most comfortable, it is as snugly shut against the outside world as a Victorian conservatory—or as Lord Emsworth's mind. "He was completely happy as only a fluffy-minded old man with excellent health and a large income can be. Other people worried about . . . strikes, wars, suffragettes, diminishing birth rates. . . . Worrying seemed to be the twentieth century's specialty. Lord Emsworth never worried . . . He was possibly as nearly contented as a human being can be in this century of alarms and excursions." [9]

In the last sixty years the people in Wodehouse have not aged one year. Lord Emsworth is an old man in 1915, but he is not a bit older in 1950, and Bertie Wooster and his friends never get out of their twenties. Young people about to be married expect to live happily ever after, timelessly, and they are quite right, for the future will be just like the present. One may say more accurately of Wodehouse's characters what Orwell said about Dickens', that they go on and on behaving like idiots in a kind of eternity.

As a comic writer in the twentieth century, Wodehouse is remarkable for his innocence and purity. A recurrent figure in the novels is the old gentleman, respected, dignified, even eminent, who once was a black sheep, the principal in scandals unmentionable even in the family circle and fatal if published. The oats that such old men sowed were apparently of the wildest strain, the deeds that they did the most dark and sinister. And what did they actually do? They got drunk, made fools of themselves, and were thrown out of pubs, music halls, and other places of entertainment. (Bertie Wooster's Uncle Percy is said to have held the record for being tossed out of Covent Garden balls.) In short, they indulged in more or less prescribed undergraduate pranks.

When one of these fellows revised the prescription, he did so not in the direction of wickedness, but in that of originality. The late Major-General Sir Miles Fish, for example, engaged in two very unmilitary engagements. First, he rode a bicycle down Piccadilly, wearing only his underclothing, in the summer of 1897. Second, he mistook the coal scuttle for a mad dog and tried to shoot it with the fire tongs in the early hours of New Year's Day of 1902. The younger generation engages in the same sort of horseplay, which is still regarded in some quarters as very serious. Thus Gussie Fink-Nottle goes wading in the fountain at Trafalgar Square and receives fourteen days without the option of a fine, together with some stern remarks from the bench.

Wodehouse is sexually pure to the point of Victorianism. There is nothing in any of the novels to bring (as a character in one of them might say) the blush of shame to the cheek of modesty. Young men are preoccupied with girls, but in a curiously sexless way. Joe Vanringham's brother Tubby began to telephone girls as soon as he could talk, but we may be sure that he never said anything unseemly. And we may be sure that he never did anything unseemly, for no young woman in Wodehouse is ever seduced, improperly fondled, or even pinched in passing. People in country houses run in and out of each other's rooms for various motives, but never for lechery. If a girl enters a young man's bedroom at midnight, his only thought is that she looks charming in her negligee.

Hollywood and the theater are just as chaste as the English country house; chorus girls are virginal, and the men who pursue them want them for their wives, not their mistresses. In a conversation about the way girls become movie stars, one character says, "If you looked into it," and the reader might expect the usual remarks about ambitious actresses sleeping with producers, but the speech continues, "you would find this Nordstrom girl was married to one of the bosses." [10] This character is called a cynic! Theatrical managers would double-cross their grand-mothers, but they do not wench. After cataloguing the crimes of the average manager (which takes about a page), Wally Mason, restricting (as the Victorians did) the area of morality to sexual matters, says: "As regards morals, that is a different matter. Most managers are respectable, middle-aged men with wives and families. They are in the business to make money, and they don't want anything else out of it." [11]

Even for gay old blades like Uncle Fred and Aunt Dahlia, marriage is a most solemn undertaking. The mere idea that a girl for whom Aunt Dahlia has real affection should marry a divorced playboy is appalling, and the idea of marrying for money is obscene. (Strangely, Wodehouse does not see anything obscene in a young woman's marriage to an old man. Billie Dore, who is still in her twenties, marries Lord Marshmoreton, who is in his fifties. That Billie is the contemporary and friend of the young man who marries Lord Marshmoreton's daughter, serves to italicize the difference between Billie's and Marshmoreton's ages, but Wodehouse gives the match his blessing.) Coveting the goods of one's neighbor is nearly universal in Wodehouse, but coveting his wife is virtually unheard of. Once Lady Julia sneeringly asks Galahad Threepwood if a young girl whom he has championed against Julia's hostility and whose mother he loved when young, is his daughter. Galahad truthfully and indignantly denies it, and the matter is over in a few moments, but there is a shock in the brief scene, for a fact out of the real world, otherwise not even mentioned by name, has suddenly been introduced.

With the exception of Aunt Dahlia's talk (and it is screened through Bertie's sense of what is fitting), Wodehouse's world is one of unusual verbal purity. Americans say, "Gosh darn it"; Englishmen say, "Dash it"; and the underworld characters of *Psmith Journalist* rasp out no stronger oath than "Gee!" Steve Jardine, a virile type who knocks around the world, prospects for gold in dangerous places, and associates with the toughest kind of human beings, says of his last, terrible trip to Columbia, "I've had a Hades of a time." [12] He is speaking to his old friend Kirk Winfield, and there are no ladies present. In recent years "hells" and "damns" have become fairly frequent, and Wodehouse even dares such compromises as "full of zip and vinegar," but his euphemisms run to the mildest varieties, "son of a what-not" probably being more common than "son of a bachelor."

III *Youth at the Prow*

Though Wodehouse's heroes are in their twenties and some of his character actors are in their sixties, they have a common state of mind which is that of the schoolboy. The splendors and miseries of school life fix the flavors and shapes of those of adult life. A fragment of school history conjures up an entire period, like Proust's *madeleine*. And a visit to the old school reduces a man to the lowly status of a new boy, at the same time bringing out in him once more a keen delight in schoolboy japes. Sneaking into a bedroom at Brinkley Court to steal back Uncle Tom's cow creamer, Bertie Wooster is reminded of the nights when he used to sneak into Aubrey Upjohn's study to pinch his biscuits. Having failed to find the cow creamer, Bertie is amazed to learn that Sir Roderick Glossop intends to go prowling around the house and find it himself. Glossop explains that as a child he played hunt-the-slipper with notable skill at Christmas parties. Furthermore, creeping through the house reminds him, with some exhilaration, of the time when he used to sneak into *his* headmaster's study to steal biscuits. This shared memory is enough to draw Bertie and the terrible Glossop into an unforeseeable chumminess. Sir Roderick tells Bertie that the biscuits at his school were mixed.

> "The ones with pink and white sugar on?"
> "In many instances, though some were plain."
> "Mine were ginger nuts."
> "Those are very good, too, but I prefer the mixed."
> "So do I, but you had to take what you could get. . . . Were you ever copped?"
> "I am glad to say never."
> "I was once. I can feel the place in frosty weather still." [13]

Bertie also remembers a time when Upjohn caught him putting sherbet in the inkwells, and the caning that followed in that instance, too. When he goes into Uncle Tom's study to talk to Upjohn, the room suddenly becomes Upjohn's study at Bramley; with Upjohn sitting behind it, the desk becomes his. It is as though Bertie were being summoned for an interview after the episode of the sherbet. Moreover, Bertie begins to see the other guests and even the host and hostess at Brinkley Court as boys under Upjohn's charge. When Aunt Dahlia ticks off Upjohn, it seems to Bertie that she has committed an unheard of piece of courage and impertinence, for which she will inevitably be punished. He only wonders whether Upjohn will order her to write out the Collect for the day ten times, or tell her to bend over for six whacks of the cane. Older and braver men than Bertie are overawed by the powers of school. Bishop Bickerton, seeing Headmaster Entwhistle in his study, dressed in cap and gown, thinks for a moment that his old schoolfellow is cutting up dangerously by putting on the cap and gown of their headmaster. The bishop is even intimidated by the older boys in the school: as he suddenly meets the football captain around a corner, his legs turn to jelly. Before he leaves the old school, however, the bishop does a bit of statue-painting.

As regards girls and small boys, the point of view of Bertie and his contemporaries is also rather like that of the schoolboy. Girls are mysterious creatures, capricious, contradictory, and unpredictable. Told that Esmond Haddock loves her after all, Corky Pirbright (says Bertie) "laughed like a hyena and also, for girls never make sense, let fall a pearly tear or two." [14] Spiritual girls are all sappy, like Madeline Bassett. Jolly girls are inclined to be boisterous, and the bond that one establishes with them may be less one of romance than one of roughhouse. Once, when dining with Lottie Blossom, Reggie Tennyson asked her to marry him. "I've never seen a girl laugh so much," he says. "It was shortly after that that she put a piece of ice down my back. I mention these things to show that we were terrific pals." [15] Small boys come under Bertie's category of pots of poison, and he has compiled a list of them with relative standings on which, for example, that amateur of the booby trap, Seabury, is above Sebastian Moon and Aunt Dahlia's Bonzo, but below Aunt Agatha's Thos.

The Wodehouse time machine also makes trips still further back, as in a story about a call that Frederick Mulliner pays on his old nurse. Pensioned by the family, Nurse Wilks still looks upon Frederick and his brother (a physician with an established practice) as boys. For Christmas, she gives them presents of books like *Eric, or Little by Little.* At the door of her cottage, Frederick is touched by the sight of the fragile old lady, until, in the voice of a sergeant major, she shouts at him to wipe his feet. He soon feels about seven years old. A former girl friend of Frederick's who has quarreled with him has come to tea, and when she says some rude things to Frederick, Nurse Wilks cuts her also down to seven-year size. When the young people squabble, she puts them in a cupboard and lets them out to finish their tea only when they promise to be good.

No other character is forced in mature life to submit to the authority of his old governess, but many of them submit to surrogate governesses, Emsworth to his sister Constance, Bertie to his two aunts, Bingo Little to his wife Rosie. In fact, any figure of authority, whether masculine or feminine, is likely enough to be seen through the eyes of childhood and take the shape of a governess. Packy Franklyn admires the beauty of Lady Beatrice Bracken, but her relish of culture and wish to dominate make him suspect, he says, that governess blood flows in her veins. Drinking cocktails, Bertie is aware that he is being watched with disapproval, and he feels as if he were "back in the Little Lord Fauntleroy suit and ringlets and having a keen-eyed governess watching one's every move like a bally hawk." [16]

Bertie's reluctance to be molded by girls who want him to read T. S. Eliot and Bergson recalls Huck Finn's reluctance to be "civilized" by the Widow Douglas. But Bertie is not as tough and resourceful as Huck, and if it were not for Jeeves, he would have to submit. But Jeeves, whose role is to protect Bertie from those authorities who would make him read serious books or stop drinking, plays a second role in which he is himself the ultimate authority. "There are moments," says Bertie in *Bertie Wooster Sees It Through,* "when he looks like a governess, one of which was this one." [17] It is in such moments, of course, that Bertie relinquishes his boyish desire for a cummerbund or a flamboyant necktie to Jeeves's conservative demands.

IV *Intellectual and Anti-Intellectual*

In spite of Wodehouse's sound education and his wide reading, Wodehouse's world is, for several reasons, anti-intellectual. First, there is a long tradition behind him. Right in the middle of the Age of Reason, Lord Chesterfield said that English gentlemen should thank God that they had something better than their brains to depend upon. Second, Wodehouse is aware that many intellectuals regard him as a literary nobody, and that many have not even bothered to look into one of his books. (The American critic John Aldridge, now an admirer, became acquainted with Wodehouse under very fortuitous circumstances: an illness and a limited library in an Alpine hotel.)

But more significant is the fact that for Wodehouse the intellectual view is equated with tragedy, pessimism, and negation. Commenting on the predicament into which one of his nephews has fallen, Mr. Mulliner says that it was as if he had stumbled into the kind of psychological novel in which the hero's soul gets tied in knots by page twenty-one and never gets straightened out again. When Mr. Mulliner suggests in another story that we leave morbidness to the Russian writers, Wodehouse is not just making a literary joke. In short, his attitude is exactly that of the man in the street, who says that there is enough sadness in life without having sad books, plays, and movies on top of it.

Most of the nice people in the novels are more or less anti-intellectual. To Lord Emsworth, the only thing worse than having a literary guest at the Castle is going to London and bringing back the blighter himself. Bertie Wooster hates going on world cruises (though Jeeves makes him go on at least one) because he hates getting mixed up with people who will drag him along on tours of cathedrals and museums. In Uncle Fred's eyes, the beautiful but literary Hermione Bostock is a mixture of Boadicea, George Eliot, and Carrie Nation. And Aunt Dahlia says of the beautiful but stupid Phyllis Mills, "I don't care what you say. Brains aren't everything. She's a dear, sweet girl. I love her like a daughter, and to hell with anyone who calls her a half-wit." [18] One of the happiest engagements in all the novels is that of Packy Franklyn and Jane Opal, each of whom was previously engaged to an intellectual; but for the grace of God, they might have been doomed to a future of going to concert halls and reading Bloomsbury novelists.

As for intellectuals themselves, after the earliest books they have replaced financiers as the least likable characters. In fact, the financier of so early a novel as *Piccadilly Jim* (1917) becomes a sympathetic character because his wife establishes a salon; poets, artists, and musicians overflow the house so that he cannot find a quiet room where he can read the Sunday papers. Leaving aside such instances as Florence Craye and Hermione Bostock, intellectuals are as short on looks as they are long on brains. Among the women of the Literary Society of Wood Hills, the pretty Adeline Smethurst stands out, Wodehouse says, like a jewel among chunks of coke. Intellectual men are small, pale, fragile, and probably physical cowards; they wear long hair and suggest by their very bearing that they are capable of writing vers libre.

In one of his golf stories, Wodehouse plays off the intellectuals against the golfers, and makes excellent comedy out of literary societies, the caprices and hypocrisies of literary fashion, the cult of the Russian novel, and his own position among critics. The community of Wood Hills has become two fiercely opposed forces, the golf club and the literary society. Applause for visiting lecturers at the home of Mrs. Smethurst causes players to foozle their shots on the nearby fairways; but badly sliced balls sail through the Smethurst windows, and one player insists on playing a niblick shot from a table around which the society is meeting. When a Russian novelist called Brusoloff comes to speak, the English writer Devine says that he is influenced by the Russian Sovietski, but Brusoloff says that Sovietski is no good. At this, women draw away from Devine, holding their skirts, and men look at him with contempt. Quickly Devine explains that he was once under the spell of Sovietski, but now he fellows Nasticoff, but Brusoloff says that Nasticoff is no good, either. Those near Devine jostle to get away from him; Mrs. Smethurst eyes him through her lorgnette; someone opens a window significantly; and the crestfallen Devine creeps out the door.

Then Brusoloff explains that the only good novelist in the world is himself: "No novelists anywhere any good except me. P. G. Wodehouse and Tolstoi not bad. Not good, but not bad. No novelists any good except me." [19] Brusoloff turns out to be a golf fan; he regards England's golfers as her greatest men, and though he has met Lloyd George, the men he most wishes to meet are Abe Mitchell and Tommy Vardon. He learns with delight that Cuthbert Banks, who has joined the literary society to court Mrs. Smethurst's niece, is the Banks who has some reputation as a golfer, and they go off to play a round. After he has got some English golf, Brusoloff intends to return to Russia, for if at home someone may throw a bomb at him, in England every member of every literary club will spring a manuscript on him.

V *Snobbery and Democracy*

Readers disagree about Wodehouse's view of the English upper classes, some considering that he satirizes them (the opinion of some of those who wished to have him hanged in the 1940's) and some considering that he snobbishly identifies himself with them (the opinion of George Orwell, for example). I should say that he does both, a bit of the first in a mild sort of way, and a good deal of the second in (as Orwell says) a rather harmless and old-fashioned way. One evidence of the snobbery is Wodehouse's love of country houses and castles. He became acquainted with them when, as a boy on holidays from school, he accompanied a clerical uncle on his rounds. Later he visited some of them for longer periods, and still later—when he became rich from his writing—he often leased one of them for part of a year or more. At Hunstanton Hall, a favorite, he used to think out stories and novels as he floated around in a boat on the castle moat.

Like Evelyn Waugh, Wodehouse likes to describe country houses and castles from various angles at different times of day. In *Something Fresh* he recounts a ride in a cart up to Blandings Castle. The approach is by winding roads past darkened cottages, black fields, and hedges, up to the massive iron gates. Then the cart takes a gravel drive through miles of park splotched with the shadows of thick shrubbery. Lights become visible here and there and then shine from a score of windows like fires on a winter's night, and at last Blandings Castle stands out against the sky like a mountain.

Castles, of course, are not only impressive physical objects; they represent a way of life, and Wodehouse finds that way attractive. To the American, George Bevan, as he looks at Belpher Castle in the distance, comes a vision of idealized feudalism. Cottages, George observes, "sat there all round the castle, singly and in groups, like small dogs round their master. They looked as if they had been there for centuries. Probably they had, as they were made of stone as solid as that of the castle. There must have been a time, thought George, when the castle was the central rallying-point for all those scattered homes; when rumor of danger from marauders had sent all that little community scuttling for safety to the sheltering walls." [20]

To be sure, life has changed at Blandings and Belpher since the Middle Ages, and Lords Emsworth and Marshmoreton might well be taken to represent the deterioration of the British governing classes. In earlier times the Emsworths were soldiers and statesmen. The ninth earl raises pumpkins and pigs, and his greatest triumphs come when his pumpkin or pig wins first prize at an agricultural show, leaving the entry of his rival, Sir Gregory Parsloe-Parsloe, in second place. Within the castle, the authority of the master is merely nominal, for his sister has usurped his place, and even his gardener disputes his orders as to what, when, and how to cultivate. Emsworth has not the slightest interest in playing host of the castle, preferring to hide out in his study and read a book on pig-breeding (Whiffle on *The Pig* is his vade mecum) while guests wander around at loose ends, cursing him. Nor has he any interest in preserving tradition (any excuse will do to avoid working on the family history) or ceremony.

Ritual has not passed from Blandings, but it is better served below stairs than above. When the family have nearly finished dinner, the upper servants go to the housekeeper's room and wait for Beach, the butler. After completing his last duties at the table, Beach joins them. Then a kitchen-maid opens the door of the housekeeper's room and announces, "Mr. Beach, if you please, dinner is served." "Mrs. Twemlow," says Beach, and, giving his arm to the housekeeper, leads the way down the passage to the Steward's Room. The rest of the servants follow them, by couples and in order of rank. [21]

The dignity and *savoir-vivre* of the aristocrat have also been transferred to the servants. Beach is perhaps the beau ideal of butlers, but butlers are generically impressive. With their slow, measured movements, their magnificent girth, and their heavy-lidded eyes, they look like Roman emperors. Among valets, Jeeves (as Bertie often tells him) stands alone. Yet a comparatively unknown valet, Webster, in *The Girl on the Boat*, exhibits extraordinary composure and courtesy when waked at three in the morning by a boor of a guest. " 'Good morning, sir,' he remarked equably. 'I fear that it will be the matter of a few minutes to prepare your shaving water. I was not aware,' said Webster in manly apology for having been found wanting, 'that you intended rising so early.' " [22]

But at the same time that he turns the English aristocracy into a joke, Wodehouse cherishes it. The Emsworth stories contain all of the staples of the mock-heroic, but Wodehouse does not mock Emsworth; he indulges the old character, and his laughter has the note of admiration that the ordinary man feels for the eccentric. Combined with his Lordship's amiability (always the saving grace in a Wodehouse character) even his fluffy-mindedness becomes likable. And Wodehouse is as impressed as any of his characters are by the self-possession of butlers and valets.

Since the self-possession of a Jeeves or a Beach is a convention of the novels, Wodehouse is delighted by the story of the butler told to him by Lord Dunsany. At the time of the Trouble in Ireland, a gang of Sinn Feiners broke down the door of a lord's house in Cork. Inside, they were met by a butler, who informed them, "His Lordship is not home." They ransacked and wrecked the house, and then they set fire to it. The flames were spreading through the house, the ceilings were about to come down, and the Sinn Feiners were leaving, when they were met again in the hall by the butler. "Who shall I say called, sir?" he asked the leader of the gang.[23]

Though the roles of master and servant are reversed in the novels, Wodehouse is no twentieth-century Beaumarchais. If Wodehouse's books actually were, as a joke of the 1930's had it, better propaganda for Communism than the works of Karl Marx, the effect of the books would be the opposite of their intent. The understanding between Bertie and Jeeves is not only pre-1789, but medieval. There is no question of Jeeves's fidelity; in Bertie's words, Jeeves can always be counted on to rally round with the feudal spirit, and in Jeeves's own, he endeavors to give satisfaction. As to Jeeves's intellectual superiority, there is nothing in the feudal view (or later views) that says that the servant should not be shrewder than the master.

Wodehouse has no time for socialistic planning or for individual socialists. In *Summer Moonshine* he describes an old country house badly rebuilt in modern style as taking on "the appearance of one of those model dwellings in which a certain number of working-class families are assured a certain number of cubic feet of air." [24] Servants with socialistic opinions are to be avoided, like Brinkley, the temporary valet who gets tight and chases Bertie with a butcher knife. Syd Price, the cockney of *If I Were You,* though not alcoholic or homicidal, is bumptious, a fact that the butler Slingsby attributes to the effects of his "Bolshie" friends. Psmith says that he is a socialist and calls everyone "comrade," but his socialism is one of his jokes, as his definition of socialism indicates. "I've just become a Socialist. It's a great scheme. You ought to be one. You work for the equal distribution of property, and start by collaring all you can and sitting on it." [25]

The novels imply that the lower classes have their place and should stay in it, and of Syd Price on a visit to Langley End, Wodehouse says unequivocally, "He wore knickerbockers, and a small and rather horrible mustache disfigured his upper lip. In his demeanor were blended the impudence and sheepishness characteristic of the Cockney who has strayed from his own familiar ground." [26] The Butler Slingsby is disgusted when Syd and his mother take advantage of the *noblesse oblige* of their betters and make themselves at home at Langley End, where Mrs. Price was once a governess. Mrs. Price is now an old sot, but in Slingsby's eyes her crime is not her drunkenness, but her presumption. Even the amiable Bertie is more comfortable when social distinctions are observed, and when he is thrown with the masses, as in a crowd at a museum or exposition, it is only about fifteen minutes, he says, until he starts feeling that he is walking on hot bricks.

Another trouble with the working classes is that instead of being dedicated to serving their betters, they are dedicated to getting money out of them. The Oldest Member says that the peasantry respond to a five-pound note as they might to a bugle call (the person of whom he speaks is, in fact, not a farmer, but a garageman). In *A Damsel in Distress* a commotion in the street brings out the irresponsibility of the working classes. "A messenger boy, two shabby men engaged in non-essential industries, and a shop girl paused to observe the scene. Time was not of the essence to these confirmed sightseers. The shop girl was late already, so it didn't matter if she was any later; the messenger boy had nothing on hand except a message marked 'Important: Rush'; and as for the two shabby men, their only immediate plans consisted of a vague intention of getting to some public house and leaning against the wall. . . ." [27]

Like Waugh, Wodehouse has a field day with the social climber and the lord whose title is but recently conferred. Sir Thomas Blunt, the director of a large store (that is, a shopkeeper) is a self-made man and is also fussy and offensive. The publisher Lord Tilbury, the ink on whose title is probably not quite dry, betrays himself by saying "Cor!" in moments of strong emotion. And at the same time that he approves of a society of stable classes with clear distinctions between them, Wodehouse makes fun of qualities in the lower classes that are inevitable results of such a society. During the performance of a play, for example, he makes mention of the battle of odors going on between the perfume in the stalls and the peppermint in the pit.

Wodehouse has as much fun with the rich American businessman as he does with the British lower orders or the commoner who has come up in the world. Like a good Tory, he reduces American efficiency to absurdity. Thus, with insane determination, the millionaire Vincent Jopp *decides* to keep his head down and drive a golf ball straight, or to marry and have a child (male) by a certain date, as he would decide to corner the wheat market. Some rich Americans speak worse English than British working people. "Say, lemme tell ya something," is a common preliminary to discussions, and Benjamin Scobell announces his plans for conquering new financial worlds by saying, "I gottan idea."

Sometimes American lack of taste reaches even to the mouth. Mr. Mulliner's chemist nephew has discovered that "if you mixed a stiffish oxygen and potassium and added a splash of trinitrotoluol and a spot of old brandy, you got something that could be sold in America as champagne at a hundred and fifty dollars the case." [28] Finally, there is a snobbery in the literary reference and quotation of the Wodehouse style, which appeals to what Aldous Huxley once called the great culture family: those people who recognize one another's allusions to Doctor Johnson, Keats, or Virgil as a family recognizes references to crusty "characters," gifted but tragic young men, and kindly old uncles of their acquaintance—while the poor outsider wonders what the devil they are talking about.

But if Wodehouse is attracted to the wealth and grace of aristocracy, he is also attracted to certain principals of democracy. Though he is something of a snob himself, he makes the snobbish characters in the novels disagreeable. He clearly dislikes Lady Underhill, who always asks who your parents were, or what regiment your uncle was in. No less clearly, he disapproves of Lady Caroline, who is disgusted because Lord Marshmoreton will not apply himself to the family history, indignant when her niece falls in love with an American to whom she has not been introduced, and outraged when her stepson exhibits certain democratic inclinations. In one novel, Wodehouse makes the point that the difference between classes is not one of blood, but one of money and what money can buy—education, leisure, travel, and so on. Tony Bryce is intelligent, well-mannered, and charming, whereas Syd Price is a barbarian; but Tony is the son of the disreputable old nanny Mrs. Price, and Syd is the proper heir to the Droitwich title. The Bassinger family, who want Tony to fight for the title that is not his, realize that the truth of the matter strikes at all of the usual assumptions of a class society.

If one adopted George Orwell's dictum that a novelist's feelings about class are always revealed by the way that he deals with marriages between classes, Wodehouse would be an unquestionable democrat. In rivalries between aristocrats and commoners, the odds are on the commoner. The successful suitor of Lady Maud is an American lyric writer, and the good and bad people are, respectively, those who want to let her marry as she is inclined to, and those who want to force her to marry an Englishman of her own class. In one of his articulate moments, Lord Marshmoreton, who belongs to the good group (as a young man he wanted to renounce the title and become a locomotive engineer or go to the United States and be a farmer), makes a speech in favor of social equality: "I don't think that the Marshmoretons are fenced off from the world by some sort of divinity. My sister does. Percy [his son] does. But Percy's an ass!" [29] By the end of the novel, his title and the protests of his sister notwithstanding, Lord Marshmoreton himself marries the American chorus girl, Billie Dore. Romance crosses class lines still another time in the same novel when Reggie Byng, the stepson of the snobbish Lady Caroline, marries Lord Marshmoreton's secretary.

For all of his joking about American crudity, Wodehouse has always liked Americans. When other young Englishmen wanted to go to the Left Bank of Paris or to the Orient, he wanted to go to the United States, because to him it was the country of romance. In one of the novels, Wodehouse makes America not only more romantic than Europe, but also morally superior. John Maude, he says, is not a bad young fellow despite the fact that his father was a decadent Mediterranean prince, for the blood of his American mother had counteracted the Mervo blood. Uncle Fred, who probably speaks for Wodehouse as much as any character can, thinks that American girls are among the wonders of the world. Sally Painter, says Wodehouse, "was just the sort of girl that appealed to him most, the sort America seems to turn out in thousands." [30]

Probably Wodehouse admires some of the qualities fostered in a democracy because he has them himself. In the first place, he is self-reliant and enterprising. He was a very young journalist when he took his vacation in the United States, sold a couple of short stories, and set out to live by free-lancing for American magazines. Second, he is hard-working. Because he has written so much and because his stories and novels run so smoothly, it might be supposed that he dashes off his work without effort. Actually, the letters to William Townend are full of comments about writing parts of a short story a dozen times, discovering that only forty out of a hundred and fifty pages of a novel are right, revising a novel by taking out two characters, and the like.

But Wodehouse enjoys work and, indeed (unlike some of his characters), he finds it a necessity. He is dismayed when he hears that Michael Arlen has retired, and he cannot imagine what Arlen does with his time. The mere idea of not writing anything for fifteen years is dreadful to a man who is frustrated when his typewriter is out of commission for three days. Finally, he combines the enterprise and the hard work with optimism. Here he reminds one of an earlier British writer who emigrated to the New World. Cheerfulness, said Robert Louis Stevenson, is the great virtue. When, at the close of World War II, Wodehouse was confined to the French hospital, he said that it was not a bad sort of life if you had a novel to write. In the hospital, in the prison camps, in the Palais de Justice in Paris—with policemen looking over his shoulder—he wrote *Uncle Dynamite,* a perfectly adequate companion piece to *Uncle Fred in the Springtime,* a novel published just before World War II broke out.

CHAPTER 7

Wodehouse and English Literature

I *Antecedents*

WODEHOUSE belongs spiritually to the world of Victoria and Edward VII, but he works in a tradition that goes back through more than three hundred years of English literature. Tracing the tradition, Lionel Stevenson points out that the themes and characters in Wodehouse have antecedents in English drama as early as Ben Jonson.[1] (For the summary of the tradition that follows and for parallels, I am indebted to Professor Stevenson.) In nearly all of Jonson's comedies there is a set of time-wasting and slangy gallants whose veracity is doubtful and whose notion of the humorous is some kind of deception, preferably with a flavor of sadism. Their chief passions are women and horse racing, and they are quite without ambition except for that of keeping on the good side of wealth. Some of them are clever enough to avoid the natural hazards of their way of life and to bring off their schemes; but others are stupid enough not only to fall into traps, but also to trip over their own feet. These gallants are usually accompanied by shrewd but unscrupulous servants. In some of Jonson's plots also there are clearly Wodehousean elements. In *The Silent Woman*, for example, two otherwise indolent young men exert themselves to help another inherit his uncle's fortune.

In Restoration comedy the gallant has evolved into the beau, more sophisticated and mannered by way of French influence, and more urbane even in the original sense of the word, for he is essentially a man of the town. He pursues women, but the pursuit is not a sentimental or romantic one so much as a companion sport to gambling and drinking. The Restoration dramatist makes a distinction between the fop who is also a clever fellow and the one who is a mere coxcomb; the latter is not knocked about as he is in Jonson, but laughed at and insulted. In the servant, too, there are some transformations. He is not so likely to be a vulgar, impudent scoundrel who cheats his master whenever he can, as he is to be prudent and trustworthy, and he may be conspicuously literate.

At its best, the comic drama of the eighteenth century preserves the wit of Restoration comedy but purges the form of its grossness, as the difference between Van Brugh's *The Relapse* and Sheridan's adaptation of it, *A Trip to Scarborough*, neatly illustrates. In the Regency the beau becomes the dandy, devoted to good food and wine, elegant clothes, gambling, flirting, worldly wisdom, epigrams, and the art of the insult.[2] In Victorian literature the dandy is very nearly absent. Dickens' portrayal of the rake in Sir Mulberry Hawk and of the foolish fop in Lord Frederick Verisopht are too exaggerated to have any credibility. More knowledgeable and more tolerant, Thackeray exhibits a somewhat degenerate specimen in the Honorable Algeron Percy Deuceace, but the heroes of the early Disraeli and Bulwer disqualify themselves because they have a streak of seriousness. Only in the lesser works of the period are there better examples, in Pierce Egan's Jerry Hawthorn and in Theodore Hook's Gilbert Gurney.

Just when it looks as if the tradition is coming to an end, Oscar Wilde revives it, with the same old scorn of bourgeois virtues, the same deception, the sadism translated into intellectual cruelty, and the epigram polished to a dazzling brightness. The influence of Wilde was dominant in the first twenty years of the twentieth century, affecting the style of writers otherwise very different from Wilde, like G. K. Chesterton, as well as the whole work of writers like Saki.

In many respects Wodehouse is remarkably close to his predecessors. Like Jonson's, his heroes are young men about town, some of them clever (Psmith, Joss Weatherby, etc.) and some of them stupid (Gussie Fink-Nottle, Freddie Threepwood, etc.). If they do not have independent incomes, they may prefer sponging on a rich relative to working. So far as their means will allow them, they cultivate fine clothes. Either with brazen confidence or with dithering timorousness, they chase girls through one novel after another. They are often devoted to gambling, usually on horses, but in the absence of a horse race, they will make do with any sort of *ad hoc* sporting proposition. Whether intelligent or stupid, they speak a language that combines classical tags, extravagant

metaphors, and catch phrases of the day. The characters secondary to the young heroes include wise servants and rich, eccentric
uncles. Typically, the action of the novels depends upon some
kind of deception, which may involve elaborate and bare-faced
lying, practical joking, or unintentional deceit through a series of
misunderstandings.

Like the writers of Restoration comedy, Wodehouse makes a
distinction between the fop who is (as the phrase in the dramatis
personae of many Restoration plays has it) "a young man of wit
and sense" and the fop who is not. To the first type, of course,
belongs Psmith, a fastidious young man whose spotless top hat
and perfectly cut morning coat impress even butlers. Like that
of the earlier fop, the fastidiousness is in part an affectation, a
stunt. Psmith professes to be greatly disturbed by the slightest im-
perfection of dress and manner, and he prides himself upon being unruffled by anything else whatsoever. In *Leave It to Psmith*
he has to wear a pink chrysanthemum to identify himself to Freddie Threepwood. (Freddie, the fool, was trying to emulate the
movies, and he meant carnation.) Complaining about the flower
as though it were some huge and hideous shrub, Psmith says that
it completely spoils his walk.

When Baxter starts throwing flower pots through the windows
of Blandings Castle, Psmith takes his time going down to investigate. Before leaving his room, he brushes his hair, selects a Hom-
burg from the hats in his closet, takes a white rose from the table,
and puts it in the lapel of his pyjamas. After his encounter with
the New York gangsters, he remarks that he now realizes the horrors of war: his hat is gone forever, having been knocked off by a
bullet, and his trousers will never be the same because he has
had to fling himself to the pavement. Even in his schooldays
Psmith has the languidness of the fop, and later he is frequently
seen sinking into soft chairs (first carefully dusted with his handkerchief) and lounging in the smoking-room windows of the
Drones Club. Psmith also has the impudence of the fop, as the advertisement that he puts in the newspapers indicates. In part, it
reads as follows:

LEAVE IT TO PSMITH!
Psmith Will Help You

Psmith Is Ready For Anything
DO YOU WANT
Someone To Manage Your Affairs?
Someone To Handle Your Business?
Someone To Take The Dog For A Run?
Someone To Assassinate Your Aunt? [3]

Psmith is no fool and no fall guy, but Bertie is something of both. Even as fop, Bertie is inferior to Psmith, for in Bertie the passion for clothes takes the form of extravagant and execrable taste. And in Bertie the languidness of Psmith becomes mere indolence and frittering away of time. His late rising, his ritual of breakfast and dressing are reminiscent of Etherege's fop without wit and sense, Sir Fopling Flutter, who regales acquaintances with an account of the strenuous morning he spends getting dressed, trying on a series of wigs, going all the way to the coffee house, and so on.

With the exception of the Mike Jackson category, Wodehouse's heroes are also like the gay blades of the Restoration, the eighteenth century, and the Regency—both on the stage and off—in their taste for the amusements and comforts of the city and their contemptuous or indifferent attitude toward the country. When Beau Brummel, who imitated art more than it imitated him, was asked which of the English lakes he liked most, he turned to his valet and asked him to remind him. "Windermere, sir," replied the valet. "Ah, yes," said Brummel, "Windermere—so it is, Windermere." [4] Bertie Wooster echoes Beau Brummel's remark in his comments on a friend who, he says, has retired to the country to wear gaiters and prod cows in the ribs and be the landed proprietor generally. Bertie himself almost never goes east of Leicester Square if he can avoid it, and any friend of his who sees him in the Covent Garden area is amazed.

Finally, there are a number of precedents for Wodehouse in the comedies of Oscar Wilde: the alias and the masquerade, the likable *flâneur*, the dragon of an aunt, the comic clergyman and the governess, three-quarters of them conducting themselves like nitwits, but all of them endowed with a fluency that outruns their intelligence, and some of them with a fund of metaphor and epigram that never fails.

Wodehouse differs from his predecessors chiefly in that he is all amiability, whereas they have at least a strain of bitterness, viciousness, or cruelty. In consequence, he has effected a reformation of the gallant and the rake. With Psmith he removes most of the inhumanity from the type, and with Bertie he removes virtually all of it. In Wodehouse the hoax is still basic, but it is the kind of hoax in which no one is actually hurt, and the epigrams are witty, but not cynical. Young men consume cocktails by the trayful, but alcohol provokes them to nothing more dissolute than barley water would. If some of the young women are tough babies, there is no Millamant in Wodehouse, much less a Hoyden.

II *Immediate Influences*

The direct influences on Wodehouse are the theater and his enormously wide reading. From his own work for the stage, Wodehouse derived the architecture and some of the materials of his novels. Richard Usborne notes that there is a distinct "three-act" feeling in many of the novels, even though the first act may be set in England, the second on a transatlantic liner, and the third in the United States. Usborne also notes that the studio of Kirk Winfield in *The Coming of Bill* appears to have been designed, not by an artist (like Kirk himself) and not by an architect, but by a dramatist—for the sake of the big scene. The studio has a kind of gallery on which the bedrooms and bath open, and the doctor and Ruth Winfield's aunt run back and forth along this gallery while Ruth lies in labor in one of the bedrooms. Downstairs, Kirk sits worrying about his wife and talking to his boxer friend. To distract Kirk, the boxer suggests that they spar for a few minutes, and next he gets the brilliant idea that he can stop Kirk's anxiety altogether by knocking him out. As Kirk falls stunned on the rug, the first cry of the baby comes from the bedroom, and the doctor and the aunt descend to treat the father.

In 1923 Wodehouse writes to William Townend that he becomes more and more convinced that a story should consist of scenes, with as little as possible between them. He also thinks of his characters as actors in a theater. He knows that major actors do not want to play a scene that is unimportant to them—though important to a supporting actor—and he believes that their objection is not mere actor's vanity, but an intuitive knowledge of stagecraft: they know that such a scene will knock the play sideways. Working on a Blandings Castle novel, he writes to Townend that Baxter needs a scene in what would correspond to the latter part of the second act.

The theater also gave Wodehouse his two greatest characters. John Hayward has read the typescript of an early sketch that Wodehouse wrote in collaboration with Herbert Westbrook, in which the manservant Barlow bears a resemblance to Jeeves. There is even a scene wherein what Bertie Wooster would call stinging words are exchanged between Barlow and his young master, Aubrey Forde-Rasche, over a question of cravats. Jeeves himself first appears in the 1917 collection of short stories called *The Man with Two Left Feet*, though only long enough to announce to Bertie that Aunt Agatha is on the premises. Two years later Wodehouse published the first four stories about Bertie and Jeeves in the collection entitled *My Man Jeeves*.

Bertie has his beginnings in that stock figure of the Edwardian stage, the Knut. Answering a letter of William Townend's, Wodehouse says, "You're absolutely right about Freddie Rooke. Just a stage dude—as Bertie Wooster was when I started writing about him. If you look at the early Jeeves stories, you'll find Bertie quite a different character now." [5] Wodehouse had used the Freddie Rooke type as early as 1910, but only as a foil to the hero. In *A Gentleman of Leisure*, Lord Dreever, with his nervous, gurgling laugh, his constant gabbling, his glassy and protruding eyes, is a literary first cousin to Bertie. It was the happy achievement of Wodehouse to take the type and make of him, in Bertie, not foil but hero.

Of the significant writers for the nineteenth-century stage, W. S. Gilbert is a major influence on Wodehouse. The constables and curates and dowagers of the Gilbert and Sullivan operas served as models for characters in the Wodehouse gallery. Gilbert's farcical methods make a general contribution, and at least one plot makes a particular contribution, a plot that Gilbert used both in *Pinafore* and *The Bab Ballads*. Far from making a secret of the fact, Wodehouse delights in calling attention to it. In *If I Were You*, the lawyer Weatherby (himself a Gilbertian lawyer), trying to make Mrs. Price recant the story that she has told about switching two babies, says: "May I remind you that this changing of one baby for another of greater rank has been the basis of a hundred *Family Herald* novelettes, and is such a stock situation in melodrama that the late W. S. Gilbert satirized it in his poem 'The Baby's Vengeance'?" [6] Tony, the supposed heir to the Droitwich title, says to Violet Waddington and her father in an earlier scene, "Well, it's like the story of 'The Baby's Vengeance' in *The Bab Ballads*. . . . Never read it? Well, there were two babies, the right one and the wrong one. I'm the wrong one." [7]

No less important than the stage is Wodehouse's reading in prose of all sorts from biography, history, and fiction to the daily newspapers, and in verse from Shakespeare to the Georgians. He reads Shakespeare through once a year; apparently he was already doing it when the Germans allowed him to take a couple of books to prison and he chose a copy of the plays as one. He knows the King James Bible backwards and forwards, and Boswell's *Life of Johnson.* Through he seems to have paid only slight attention to the poets of the eighteenth century, he has a very close acquaintance with the Romantics and the Victorians. From boyhood he read Dickens, and late in life he began to read Trollope. He probably knows Arthur Conan Doyle's work as well as any Baker Street Irregular, and he must know more of the sheer trash of the Victorian and Edwardian ages than any other man now alive.

Nor does Wodehouse neglect the literature that follows. He reads Somerset Maugham and Aldous Huxley (though after buying *Brave New World,* he could not read it; he felt that a man who wrote so well about the present was wasting his time writing about the future). Apparently he has read Evelyn Waugh from the beginning for, writing to Townend in the forties of the brilliance of *Put Out More Flags*, he also says that *Decline and Fall* was a masterpiece of a novel. He feels about Waugh as a comic writer what Bertie feels about Jeeves, that he stands alone. But he admires Priestly and wishes that he could write a novel like *The Good Companions.* Later he takes up the work of George Orwell and T. H. White. Moreover, he reads scores of books by lesser known writers and by writers now quite unknown: Warwick Deeping, David Mackail, J. D. Beresford, Claude Houghton, E. V. Lucas, and W. B. Maxwell.

Though Wodehouse does not ignore American literature, he reads less of it than he does of British. Some of it (like William

Faulkner's *Sanctuary*, which he says gave him the horrors, made him feel sick) is too strong for him. But he enjoys the detective story writers—Raymond Chandler, Rex Stout—and the humorists and wits—James Thurber, Damon Runyon, Dorothy Parker. When he is disappointed in what the English and American writers are doing, he turns to the French, reading all of Colette, including her autobiography, *Mes Apprentissages,* and Desparbe's *Les Demi-Soldes* (a story about the plot to bring the son of Napoleon to the throne). He ranges through all manner of periodicals and, indeed, he seems to have that passion for printed matter that led H. L. Mencken to read everything that came before his eyes, even prospectuses for stock companies.

The first use that Wodehouse makes of his reading in major writers is imitation and parody: imitation in the early books and parody in the later, though it may be impossible to draw a distinct line, since Wodehouse may not have been sure himself which he wanted to write at one stage. In *The Pothunters* the detective sent from London speaks a dialect of Dickens, the idiom of Mr. Jingle. Of a boy kleptomaniac in a previous case, he says: ". . . advised the father to send him to one of those North Country schools where they flog. Great success. Stole some money. Got flogged instead of expelled. Did it again with same result. Gradually got tired of it. Reformed character now." [8]

In *A Gentleman of Leisure* the name Spike connotes the Bowery, where the character comes from, but it also echoes Spike in *Nicholas Nickleby;* Jimmy Pitt plays a kind of Nicholas to Spike, and the chapter in which he finds Spike, who has fled from the United States and is down and out in London, is entitled "Jimmy Adopts a Lame Dog." The butler Beach, who will not give the same advice to Ronnie Fish in the drawing room as he will in the pantry, borrows this distinction from *Great Expectations,* where Wemmick talks to Pip in one way in Little Britain and in another at Walworth. From Dick Swiveller in *The Old Curiosity Shop,* Wodehouse gets the trick of quoting verse as prose, as well as (Usborne observes) some of Swiveller's favorite quotations. [9]

After a brief period of imitation, Wodehouse uses lesser writers and writers of obvious trash for purposes of parody. Both the adult characters and the boys of the first school stories are modeled on the traditional types and reflect the traditional loyalties;

but before he has stopped writing school stories, Wodehouse has started to make little jokes about school, and later he makes a joke of the whole business. "After all, Mulliner," says Bishop Bickerton, "to whatever eminence we may soar, howsoever great may be the prizes which life has bestowed upon us, we never wholly lose our sentiment for the dear old school. It is our Alma Mater, Mulliner, the gentle mother that has set our hesitating footsteps on the—." "Absolutely," said Augustine.[10]

In the early romances Wodehouse takes the traditional situations more or less seriously; in the later ones he makes fun of them and goes right on using them. Joe Vanringham is not at all discouraged when Jane Abbott tells him that she is already engaged to another man, for in the manuscripts that he used to read at Busby's, the heroine was always engaged to someone else at the start of the story. Similarly, when Joss Weatherby, posing as a valet, tells the butler Chibnail that he is a nobleman disowned by his father for refusing to marry the girl his father has chosen for him, Chibnail instantly understands; for the situation is one that he has encountered in such bilge fiction as *Hyacinth, Mark Delamere, Gentleman,* and *The World Well Lost.* In the short stories, Wodehouse likes to parody not only the plots of the sentimental novelette, but also (sometimes at length) the style. Colonel Carteret, in love with his young ward, says to the man whom he imagines to be his rival: "Go to her, my boy, go to her, and don't let any thought of an old man's broken dream keep you from pouring out what is in your heart. I am an old soldier, lad, an old soldier. I have learned to take the rough with the smooth. But I think—I think I will leave you now. I—I should like to be alone for a while. If you need me you will find me in the raspberry bushes." [11]

With melodrama, Wodehouse runs the same course as he does with the sentimental novel. In the earliest books he writes quite seriously, for instance, of people in the stress of strong emotion gripping a table until their knuckles whiten under the strain. Later, he puts melodrama on his comic roller coaster, sometimes taking along a cargo of popular Gothic as well. In one of the Mulliner stories there is a butler called Murgatroyd (the same name that Gilbert used for the noble family in *Ruddigore*); a proud and sinister baronet; a beautiful girl locked in an upstairs room; and a hero who disguises himself so that he can rescue her. "And presently . . . there came to his ears from an upstairs window a sound that made him stiffen like a statue and clench his hands till the knuckles stood out white under the strain. It was the sound of a woman sobbing." [12]

But Wodehouse's reading has a more important result in the formation of the whole fabric of his prose style. The prose of the novels and short stories is always a pleasure and frequently a delight. (Curiously, that of the occasional essays is not so successful. The movement of narrative is required to spark the style, and when, as now and then in the earliest novels, he digresses into the essay to comment or generalize, Wodehouse can fall into a *longueur*. Yet even in the school stories he writes passages that anticipate the mature style. Reporting the discussion between Mike Jackson and a Dulwich landlady, he says, "Having stated these terms, she dribbled a bit of fluff under the bed . . . and relapsed into her former moody silence." [13])

The style is admirably clear, though it is one of mad and marvelous variegation. Slang goes hand in hand with archaic words and with unfamiliar words that one might have imagined to have been patented by James Branch Cabell. Exotic terms jostle technical ones, so that the distance between English villages is measured in parasangs, and fiction is described as stearine. Queer words come out of crossword puzzles, and synonyms spill out of the thesaurus. It is perfectly natural for a character to reply to an inquiry about the health of an aunt, "Ticking over reasonably well, though copping it to a certain extent with rheumatic pangs," or to identify a girl, in the idiom of *Who's Who,* as "Clarissa, only daughter of Colonel Anstruther Boote, D.S.O., and Mrs. Boote of Simla Lodge, Wimbledon Common." [14]

The vocabulary is not only a matter of words, but also one of phrases from the various sports, trades, professions, and disciplines, and of quotations from standard and substandard works of literature. Wodehouse likes to have one character tell another that he will reduce him to the status of a third-class power, or to remark that the servants at a country house have downed tools. Still more vital to the prose is the interpolation of the snatches from literary works. In the earliest books, as a young man fresh from school, Wodehouse inclined to quotations from Horace and other

Latin writers (some in the original), as well as from Shakespeare and other English writers. Later, he tends to make a minimal use of authors other than English, as probably too pretentious and too difficult to fit into the mosaic of his syntax.

From the very beginning, Wodehouse uses bits of Shakespeare. When a boy is out of the cricket team with chickenpox, another asks, like Hamlet addressing the skull of Yorick, where are his drives now, his cuts that were wont to set the pavilion in a roar? When Mike's friend Wyatt is caught breaking out at night—and knows that he will have to leave school—he tells Mike that they will meet at Philippi, later a favorite rendezvous of Bertie and Jeeves and others. Throughout the romantic and the comic novels and the short stories, the quotations from Shakespeare come thick and fast, and they are attributed to one and all. The steward, Albert Peasemarch has the following impression of Monty Bodkin when Monty discovers that the toy Mickey Mouse, in which a necklace has been secreted, is missing: "Even such a man, so faint, so spiritless, so woebegone, drew Priam's curtain in the dead of night and would have told him half his Troy was burnt." [15]

When the butler Chibnail catches Vera Pym, his barmaid fiancée, straightening the tie of a commercial traveler, he is, Joss Weatherby reports, greatly upset: "Oh curse of marriage, he said to himself, that we can call these delicate creatures ours, but not their appetites. His impulse was to write her a stinker." [16] As befits his dignity, Jeeves quotes more of Shakespeare than any other character. Bertie says that if he executes the latest larcenous mission that Aunt Dahlia has given him, he will probably be caught, and Jeeves replies: "I quite understand, sir. And thus the native hue of resolution is sicklied o'er with the pale cast of thought, and enterprises of great pitch and moment in this regard their currents turn awry and lose the name of action." "Exactly," says Bertie, "you take the words out of my mouth." [17]

In the letters to Townend, Wodehouse expresses a poor opinion of seventeenth-century drama, but he quotes Otway's outburst on women several times, and he borrows occasional oaths from Etherege and other comic writers ("stap my vitals"). From the eighteenth century he takes comparatively little, but there are familiar bits of Gray ("full many a gem," etc.) and discriminating pieces of Sheridan ("a damned disinheriting countenance").

Wodehouse quotes wholesale from the Romantics. As Lord Emsworth watches his prize pig eat heartily, his heart leaps up like Wordsworth's, and when James Duff gets an idea for marketing hams, he is like something out of "Kubla Khan": ". . . J. B. Duff did not get ideas, he got obsessions, and on these occasions was like the gentleman in the poem who on honeydew had fed and drunk the milk of paradise. You just said, 'Beware, beware! His flashing eyes, his floating hair!' and wove a circle round him thrice and that was practically all you could do about it." [18] People frequently look at each other with a wild surmise and call for beakers full of the warm South, and Joss Weatherby quotes a long section of "Ode to a Nightingale." He explains that he and Howard Steptoe were in the garden in the middle of the night, not to rob the house but to hear the nightingale, and Steptoe confirms his account, which runs in part thus: "We could not see what flowers were at our feet, nor what soft incense hung upon the boughs, but we managed to catch a glimpse of the bird, did we not, sir?" "Yeah," replies Mr. Steptoe, "it was a whopper." [19]

Of the Victorian poets, Wodehouse quotes most frequently from Tennyson, having a special affinity for the caste of Vere de Vere and the superiority of kind hearts to coronets and simple faith to Norman blood—but not neglecting the curse that came upon the Lady of Shalott and the tenfold strength of Galahad. He also draws upon Browning, Swinburne, Fitzgerald, the Rossettis, and Arnold, and also from less significant poets—Henley, for instance. In fact, Wodehouse has a partiality for some of the minor poets, such as Hood, and the number of characters whom he describes as having, like Eugene Aram, gyves upon their wrists, includes not only a quorum of the Drones Club, but also Lottie Blossom's dog.

As to prose, Wodehouse may quote anything from the well-known statement of General Grant about fighting it out along this line to the less familiar remark of a Prussian field marshal on London (Blucher's "What a city to loot!") to the dying words of a German writer (bewildered by the developments of the plot, Monty Bodkin calls, like Goethe, for more light). Most of the prose quotations, however, come from fiction, and one of the favorite sources is the Sherlock Holmes cycle. When he begins to relate his adventures, Bertie often employs the language of Doctor

Watson. For instance, in the opening paragraph of the story "Jeeves Makes an Omelet," Bertie tells the reader that if anyone should ever found a society for keeping aunts in check and ask him to join, he would do so instantly, "And my mind would flit to the sinister episode of my Aunt Dahlia and the Fothergill Venus. . . ." [20] Elsewhere, Bertie refers to the sinister affairs of Sir Watkyn Bassett and Bertie's visit to Bassett's house in Gloucestershire, and of Sir Watkyn and the silver cow creamer. Or, juggling Watson's idiom and his own, he explains that certain events took place "about half a dozen years ago, directly after the rather rummy business of Florence Craye, my Uncle Willoughby's book, and Edwin, the Boy Scout." [21]

Like Holmes in the early stages of a case, Wodehouse's characters remark that these are deep waters, or that the matter presents certain points of interest. Bertie, Bobbie Wickham, and others say, as someone approaches, that this, if they mistake not, is our client now. Various characters ask various others to put the facts before them, omitting no detail, however slight. Like Holmes talking to Watson, Psmith tells Mike that he knows his methods, and one of Mr. Mulliner's nephews, required to spend an evening with his hard-drinking publisher, who usually ends his revels in jail, says that he has stern work before him.

The conclusion of one of the short stories parodies the conclusions of some of the Sherlock Holmes stories, in which, having solved the case, Holmes suggests that he and Watson go to the Albert Hall or Covent Garden to hear some music. At the end of "The Adventure of the Red Circle," for instance, Holmes and Watson hurry off to be in time for the second act of a Wagner opera. At the end of Wodehouse's "The Word in Season," Bingo Little, having got out of one of his scrapes without his wife's learning about it, says to Mr. Purkiss, "But come, let us go and listen to Algeron Aubrey [Bingo's infant son, who has just spoken the word "cat," though he was pointing to the picture of a rhinoceros when he spoke it] on the subject of Cats. They tell me he is well worth hearing." [22]

Wodehouse uses, deliberately and ironically, the stockpile of clichés that he has accumulated from his reading. Victims are stabbed in libraries with paper knives of oriental design; whispers go round clubs; toads by the gross crouch beneath harrows;

young men tread the primrose path (unless they give it the miss in baulk), and people of all ages stiffen like statues. As Bertie Wooster considers the possible consequences of the fact that Gussie Fink-Nottle, engaged to Madeline Bassett, is falling in love with Corky Pirbright, his soul is darkened with a nameless fear. At an earlier time in his life, it was darkened when he was informed that the Reverend Aubrey Upjohn wished to see Wooster in his study after evening prayers. As the publisher Lord Tilbury begins to recover from the cancellation of a profitable contract and an unpleasant interview with the formidable Lady Julia, life steals back into his rigid form. When Tilbury fires Monty Bodkin, Monty leaves the office with the air of a French aristocrat stepping into the tumbril.

Wodehouse's reading also provides him with a store of allusions. He draws upon his studies at Dulwich for references to *The Odyssey*, Xenophon's *Ten Thousand*, Apuleius' *The Golden Ass* and Juvenal. School, together with later reading, furnishes references to the Bible (Jael, the wife of Heber, is a favorite figure), Abelard and Heloise, Edith and Harold, and Judge Jeffreys. There are, of course, a great many references to Dickens (Sidney Carton, the Cherryble Brothers, the Artful Dodger, Dotheboys Hall, etc.). With this sort of allusion, Wodehouse mingles allusions to current affairs and to people popular in the theater and movie worlds. (Stiffy Byng is said to be a girl of about the size of Jessie Matthews.) And he likes this sort of mixture to describe a young man, wondering what has happened to his fiancée, who has gone to London to see his guardian about getting his money: ". . . his frame of mind resembled in almost equal proportions that of Mariana in the Moated Grange and that of those priests of Baal who gashed themselves with knives." [23]

Finally, to the orchestration of his style, with its classical themes, its clichés, its parodies and echoes, Wodehouse adds his special brand of metaphor. Some of the metaphors are merely ingenious hyperbole or understatement. On the one hand a sensitive golfer misses putts because of the terrible racket made by the butterflies in the meadow next to the course, and on the other an Englishman buzzes over to Canada for the salmon fishing. At other times Wodehouse adapts the metaphor to the situation, as Bob Acres with his "referential" swearing; thus a girl in one of the golf stories is so beautiful that she makes other women look like battered repaints. The figures are often madly incongruous; Bingo Little's infant son not only has the aspect of a mass murderer, but that of a mass murderer suffering from an ingrown toenail. And frequently the figures are skillfully mixed, as in Bertie Wooster's remark that the rumpuses that Bobbie Wickham is always starting may be amusing to her, but not to the unfortunate toads beneath the harrow whom she ruthlessly plunges into the soup. In addition to all of this, there are a few minor devices of style and eccentricities. As regards verbs, people do not walk, but trot, toddle, slide, beetle, and so on. And Wodehouse likes nonce abbreviations like "the bacon and e," "a stately home of E," and "eight hours of the dreamless."

III *Old Pro*

Wodehouse is one of the most prolific and one of the most popular writers of the twentieth century. Fred Allen (probably having cast a cold eye over row upon row of radio scripts) once said that he was the only man who had written more than he could lift, but Wodehouse has written more than Allen wrote, perhaps more than Allen and his teams of writers did. When John Lardner was in London during the 1930's, he bought at Herbert Jenkins ten or twelve Wodehouse novels that he had not found in America. The lady who sold them to him said that the only trouble with Wodehouse was that he wrote books so fast that he produced a new one before the demand for the previous one had slackened. In *Over Seventy*, published in 1957, Wodehouse says that he has written ten boys' books, one children's book, forty-three novels, three hundred and fifteen short stories, four hundred and eleven articles, and written or collaborated on sixteen plays and sixteen musical comedies. Since then he has published five novels and a book of short stories, and he is still publishing stories in magazines. If there were an association to study Wodehouse's work, as the Baker Street Irregulars study the Sherlock Holmes stories, its members would have plenty to occupy them.

More surprising than the vast amount of work that Wodehouse has done is the care with which he has done it. The caricature by Low on the dust jacket of Richard Usborne's book, a big smile on Wodehouse's face and his hands in his pockets, might suggest that Wodehouse is the Rossini of the light novel. But Usborne's title, *Wodehouse at Work*, and the photograph of the frontispiece, Wodehouse at his typewriter, tell the truth. In *Over Seventy* Wodehouse says that he hopes that when he is dead and people are telling each other what a rotten writer he was, one voice will be raised to say that at least he took trouble. Part of the trouble he takes is a very thorough planning of his books. "It has always seemed to me," he remarks in *Over Seventy*, "that planning a story out and writing it are two separate things. If I were going to run a train, I would feel that the square thing to do was to provide the customers with railway lines and see that the points were in working order." If he did not, he continues, the reader might well shout out like the lady in Marie Lloyd's song:

> Oh, mister porter,
> What shall I do?
> I want to go to Birmingham,
> And they're taking me on to Crewe.[24]

The typescript of *Jeeves in the Offing*, for example, is accompanied by seventy pages of pencilled notes, each page dated and the lot of them covering twenty-three months. They are the record of the process by which Wodehouse thought out the novel, talking to himself, putting down tentative data, making suggestions to himself, marking a point with approval.[25] On the details of the story, Wodehouse works equally hard. While writing *Sam the Sudden,* he asks William Townend, an old hand on tramp steamers, for some technical information. Sam is standing outside the galley of the tramp steamer. How should he be dressed? What does he see, hear, smell? In what capacity would he have had to sail on a previous voyage to know the skipper? How long is the average voyage from the United States to England? Townend answered all of the questions, but in the end Sam never stood outside the galley.

Between the pencilled notes and the text of the novel, Wodehouse writes a "scenario" of about thirty thousand words. This enables him to avoid holes in the plot and also gives him ideas for dialogue, which he puts down in skeleton form and works up later. Now he can proceed with the first draft, sometimes writing two or three thousand words a day. In *Bring On the Girls,* Guy Bolton tells about a device that Wodehouse employed to feed a roll of paper into his typewriter, so that he would not have to lose momentum by taking one sheet out and putting another in the machine. At the end of the day he would cut the roll into pages and pin them on the wall; then he walked around and read through the day's work. Where the story appeared to sag, he pinned the page lower, and where it needed a twist, he pinned it crooked. Next he revised until he could pin all the pages straight and level again.

The story is probably a joke, but it is a joke that has at least a factual foundation.[26] However rapidly he writes, Wodehouse does an immense deal of rewriting. He tells Townend of the difficulty that he had with the early chapters of *Heavy Weather,* a sequel to *Summer Moonshine,* because he had to bear in mind the people who had not read the earlier book, and at the same time avoid explanations that would bore the people who had. To get a hundred pages of the novel, he estimates, he wrote a hundred thousand words. Writing *The Mating Season,* a Bertie and Jeeves story, in 1946, he regrets that he does now only three pages a day, whereas he once did eight. But the Bertie and Jeeves books take longer than the others, he says, because every word has to count. He even rewrites stories after submission. Once he wrote an Ukridge story which he felt was not quite right, and *Redbook* confirmed his feelings by rejecting it. He rewrote it as a Bingo Little story, and the *Post* took it.

Wodehouse's attitude, as well as his method of work, is that of a lifelong professional. Reading in Trollope's *Autobiography* the celebrated account of how the great Victorian wrote two hundred and fifty words per quarter hour during his morning stint, Wodehouse does not simply say, as people usually do, that the feat is incredible or enviable. He cannot believe that anyone could possibly sit down and write an intricate novel like *Is He Popenjoy?* with such speed unless he had planned it minutely. But if it were planned, there would be nothing remarkable about writing fifteen hundred words each morning. For he himself sits down to work each day after breakfast, whether or not he feels at the top of his form, and before he gets up, he has written just about as much as Trollope did. He has no respect for one-story and one-book writers. Looking at American magazines in 1949, he says that more and more fiction appears to be written by people who do one or two stories and then sink without a trace. In 1929 he says that two-thirds of the novels being published are written by one-book novelists. The test of a writer is whether he can write three novels. Yet Wodehouse is also an amateur, in the original sense of the word, a man who writes out of sheer love of writing. In the spring of 1945 he tells Townend that he is not greatly worried whether the books that he wrote during the war will be published. He has got them down on paper, and he can reread them and revise them and improve them.

It would be silly to deny that there is a substantial amount of repetition as regards plots and characters in Wodehouse's work. (This repetition may account for the feeling that some readers have got that Wodehouse has written himself out at one stage or another. Wodehouse has written some of his best books and some of his run-of-the-mill books in the same periods, but there has been no decline in his powers. When a reader thinks that he has seen a decline, the likelihood is that he has been reading too much Wodehouse at one time.) The very titles of some of the books—*Summer Moonshine* and *Summer Lightning, Heavy Weather* and *Hot Water, Uncle Fred in the Springtime* and *Uncle Dynamite*—suggest repetitiousness. The books under these titles are not, in fact, sets of twins, but they might serve as an indication of the consistency of Wodehouse's plots, characters, settings, and themes.

Beyond this, however, there is some marked self-borrowing and reworking. *Spring Fever* and *The Old Reliable* are much the same story, aside from the fact that one is set in an English country house and the other in a large Hollywood house. Richard Usborne explains that after *Spring Fever* was published, Edward Everett Horton asked Wodehouse for a play with a good butler part in it for himself, and so Wodehouse turned the novel into a play, adapting it for American audiences. Then it turned out that Horton could not use the play. Wodehouse, therefore, had a script on his hands, and he thought that it was different enough from the original novel to make a new one out of it.

Psmith Journalist is not much more than *The Prince and Betty* with the love story and the scenes on the made-up Mediterranean island left out. In *Psmith Journalist* as in *The Prince and Betty*, the editor of a soppy magazine goes on vacation, and the assistant editor turns the magazine into a sports and crusades journal, touting a boxer who deserves a break and exposing a slum landlord who deserves to be broken. There is a switch of sorts: in the first novel an athletic hero joins a foppish, monocle-wearing "socialist" editor, Rupert Smith, whereas in the second novel the foppish, monocle-wearing "socialist" Psmith joins the athletic editor, Billy Windsor. Otherwise, *Psmith Journalist* runs on the same rails that Wodehouse put down for *The Prince and Betty*. The magazine *Peaceful Moments* becomes *Cozy Moments*, but the names of the features and of the contributors do not change. The same boxer, office boy, and good and bad gangsters play the same parts.

Sometimes, however, Wodehouse reworks not because he does not wish to waste something, but because he wants to improve something. The short story called "Unpleasantness at Kozy Kot," published in a 1959 collection, is a rewriting of the story called "Fixing It Up For Freddie," published in a 1925 collection, and it is a much better story than the earlier one. Wodehouse adds a complication to the plot, so that instead of winning the girl he did in "Fixing It Up For Freddie" the hero loses her, but thereafter wins a parson's daughter.

Wodehouse wants no part of one kind of repetition, that within a story or novel. The *Ladies' Home Journal* offered him forty-five thousand dollars for what it thought was a good project, a modern version of *Helen's Babies*, but Wodehouse refused the offer because he could see no way of getting around the monotony of the original structure. In the days when *Helen's Babies* was published, it may have been all right to take one idea and build upon it a series of incidents in which the children get into trouble. But it would never do now; at least Wodehouse does not wish to do it. His own novels are rich in incident, and even the short stories are sufficiently complex. In the golf stories and the Mulliner stories and others, Wodehouse generously furnishes a prologue which itself requires a measure of invention before he proceeds to the narrative proper. In the opening section of one story, a Bean at the Drones Club asks Oofie Prosser to go to a wrestling match, and Oofie, after recoiling in horror, makes a speech denouncing wrestlers and leaves the smoking room in disgust. Thereupon a Crumpet tells the story, which explains why Oofie was so horrified.

Even run-of-the-mill stories have several high points. For example, Augustine Mulliner, a diffident young curate, takes a bottle of tonic invented by his uncle and sent to him by his aunt, who has noticed that he looks pale and thin. The tonic stimulates him to such aggressive confidence that he wins his girl, despite the fact that she is the daughter of his vicar, the terrible Stanley Brandon. Then he incites his hen-pecked bishop to defy his wife, and is rewarded with the position of secretary to the bishop. Next he receives a letter from his uncle, saying that his well-meaning aunt has made a dreadful mistake. The tonic is compounded in two forms, one for run-down human beings and one for elephants who are inclined to hang back a little on Indian tiger hunts. Hence, Augustine should in no case take any of the tonic. But Augustine's reply to the letter is a telegram asking his uncle to send him three cases of the formula for elephants.

IV *Significance*

The obiter dicta of other writers, criticism (some of it also by other writers), and the attention paid to him in reference works are all, in one way or another, indexes of a writer's importance. Within the guild of writers, Wodehouse has a majority of supporters and a somewhat peevish minority. Sean O'Casey, a member of the latter, called Wodehouse the performing flea of English literature, an insult which, of course, Wodehouse blandly turned into the title of his book of letters. E. C. Bentley, the author of detective stories and the inventor of the light verse form called (after his middle name) the clerihew, protested that Oxford University had given a Doctor of Letters to a fellow who was a mere humorist without a single serious line to his credit.

On the other hand, three generations of the Waugh family have admired Wodehouse as a great comic writer. In a 1935 letter to Wodehouse, Arthur Waugh says that he used to read Wodehouse's books with Alec when Alec was a schoolboy, and that in their letters to each other they still fall into Psmithisms. He can truly say that, emulating Wolfe, he would rather have created Psmith than have stormed Quebec. Both Evelyn and Auberon

Waugh regard Wodehouse as the master of comic novelists in this century. Hilaire Belloc once called Wodehouse the best of living English writers, a comic novelist who uses the means of his craft with such skill that he frequently reaches perfection. (Hugh Walpole was envious of the tribute, and when they met at Oxford, Walpole asked whether Wodehouse had heard what Belloc had said about him. Wodehouse had. Then Walpole remarked that he wondered why Belloc had said such a thing, and Wodehouse replied that he wondered too. After a long silence Walpole said that he could not imagine why Belloc had said what he had; Wodehouse acknowledged that he could not either. Another long silence, and Walpole said that the remark was most extraordinary. Most extraordinary, Wodehouse agreed. There was a third silence, during which Walpole apparently arrived at a satisfactory solution to the mystery. "Ah, well," he said, "the old man's getting very old." [27]) J. B. Priestly, Anthony Powell, and other writers have also praised Wodehouse as a superb writer, a prince of entertainers, and a comic poet. Powell calls him a genius, in his way.

Wodehouse has provoked only a small body of criticism, but to this one should probably apply a sliding scale, for no comic writer is likely to attract as much comment as a "serious" one. As all actors are said to wish to play Hamlet, criticism has always been challenged by tragedy. Even when it does not take up the challenge of tragedy in the strict sense of the term, it feels most responsible when it is at work on grave subjects. Recent history has made the inclination sharper in our time than in most. The events of the last half century have been cruel indeed, and sometimes it seems as if all literature should be real and earnest. Anguish becomes the identity card of the writer. For every article published on (for instance) the fine comic novelist, Marcel Aymé, a couple of dozen are published on one of the French existentialists, though for all his fantasy Aymé is never far from the real world. Wodehouse, of course, is very far; and John W. Aldridge has suggested additional reasons for the scantiness of criticism on Wodehouse, to which I shall refer later.

The only book on Wodehouse besides this one is Richard Usborne's *Wodehouse at Work*, which I have already cited a number of times. Usborne has read Wodehouse for more than forty years; he has gone through virtually all of the collected work, and he has gone back to read some of Wodehouse's earliest adventure stories for magazines. On the one side, the result is a knowledge of Wodehouse's development, the formulas on which he relies, and the cycles which much of his work comprises (Blandings Castle, Bertie and Jeeves, etc.). On the other, it is a knowledge of the qualities in Wodehouse that sustain the cycles and make the work durable in spite of the formulas.

Because Usborne corresponded with Wodehouse and talked with friends of Wodehouse in England, *Wodehouse at Work* is the best source of biographical information, next to *Performing Flea* and *Over Seventy*. Indeed, it has material on Wodehouse's family and on Dulwich that Wodehouse's own books do not. Since Usborne is himself British, he is better equipped than an American writer to deal with Wodehouse's school years. To *Wodehouse at Work*, there are valuable appendices that include not only a bibliography of the novels and books of short stories, but also a list of the plays and musicals that Wodehouse wrote alone or in collaboration. (One learns that though little of Wodehouse's own script writing reached the screen, twenty-two of his books were transferred to film by other writers, and that *A Gentleman of Leisure* and *Piccadilly Jim* were filmed twice.) An appendix on "The French for Wodehouse" demonstrates that translating Wodehouse into other languages is a skull-breaking and sometimes impossible task. For those readers who know Latin, Usborne reproduces the address of the Public Orator at the conferring of Wodehouse's degree by Oxford.[28]

In his critical survey, *The Georgian Scene* (1935), Frank Swinnerton gives Wodehouse high marks for his invention of comic episode (on which, rather than his idiom, his popularity outside English-speaking countries must depend). But he pays his greatest tribute to Wodehouse as the inventor of a language—a language which he considers to be not English so much as pure nonsense. Wodehouse's verbal gymnastics are clearly superior to those of any other English writer now living. If nothing else, Wodehouse is what Doctor Johnson would call a public benefactor for, more than any other writer of his time, he has brought laughter and happiness to people of all classes. Swinnerton also quotes the statement that another writer made to him after reading a Wodehouse story in *Strand:* Wodehouse, said Arnold Bennett, was a far abler writer than any of the highbrow novelists of the day.[29]

John Hayward's essay on Wodehouse in *The Saturday Book,* 1941–1942, furnishes important biographical data, makes suggestions about influences on Wodehouse's work, and discusses the work itself. Perhaps the most illuminating part of the essay is the section on Wodehouse's development, which Hayward shows was remarkably early and rapid (though Wodehouse modestly feels that he was a slow learner). Much of the material for the later books is present in the school novels. In the first of them Wodehouse is already writing the dialogue that *The Spectator* called excellent at the time, and in the second school novel, Reginald Farnie is a recognizable model for two Wodehouse types, the *enfant terrible* and the *boulevardier.*

By the time of *Tales of St. Austin's,* the Wodehouse manner is evident in the opening sentence of "Bradshaw's Little Story": "The qualities which in later years rendered Frederick Wackerbath Bradshaw so conspicuous a figure in connection with the now celebrated affair of the European, African, and Asian Pork Pie and Ham Sandwich Supply Company frauds were sufficiently in evidence during his school career to make his masters prophesy gloomily concerning his future." [30] In 1910, says Hayward, Wodehouse published a novel that not only indicated what the materials of his later books would be, but also revealed some of their arrangements and their laws—the elements of both melodrama and musical comedy, the tensions between the old and the young, the lovers initially star-crossed but eventually happy. Moreover, this novel, *A Gentleman of Leisure,* shapes with a good deal of accuracy the outlines of the Blandings Castle novels. One of the settings is a stately home of England, and one occasion of the action is the first of the many house parties in the novels. The characters include: peers old and young (in the latter genus, Lord Dreever is also an obvious species of Drone); independently rich people; a self-made millionaire; shady characters out to double-cross each other; a tartar of an aunt; a nitwit of a girl; a man-about-town, and a butler.[31]

In his essay "In Defense of P. G. Wodehouse," written in 1945, George Orwell is advocate first and critic second, but in the submission of his evidence that Wodehouse was innocent, he makes some shrewd critical observations. For example, he notes that the atmosphere of Wodehouse's novels has not changed since 1925, and that all of the characters by whom Wodehouse is best known appeared before that date: Psmith in 1909, Lord Emsworth and others of the Blandings Castle saga in 1915, and Bertie and Jeeves in 1917. Even when Wodehouse began to write about him, Bertie was out of date, for he is the "Knut" of the pre-World War I period, the subject of songs like "Gilbert the Filbert" and "Reckless Reggie of the Regent's Palace." Orwell also notices that Wodehouse does not satirize the Establishment, that he accepts it as he accepts the code of the schoolboy. Though he exploits the comic possibilities of the aristocracy, the line of barons and earls that begins with Lord Emsworth is merely ridiculous, not immoral or contemptible. Only a non-English reader could make the mistake of thinking that Wodehouse attacks the aristocracy, of failing to see that Emsworth is funny in part because an earl should have dignity, and that Bertie is funny because the master should not be inferior to the servant.[32]

In a piece for *The New Yorker,* John Lardner makes a brief survey of Wodehouse's work to 1948. He believes that *Spring Fever,* published that year, represents a decline in Wodehouse's powers, and he thinks that he has noticed some failing of power once or twice before. Having looked at the earlier work again, he concludes that there are three periods in Wodehouse. The first is that of the light novels of love and adventure; the second that of the comedies, in which Wodehouse found himself; the third period is one in which Wodehouse goes through the motions of the second. But Lardner still regards Wodehouse as a writer who, at his best, has a comic gift rich enough to make the reader laugh out loud.[33]

Lionel Stevenson, in his article on the antecedents of Wodehouse, concedes that if marked variety and growth are necessary qualities of greatness, Wodehouse is no great writer. For he achieved his kind of perfection early and has not changed or experimented. But his consistency is part of his attraction: he can be counted on to do what we have long expected of him. Furthermore, in creating two or three characters who are familiar to the whole reading public, he can claim to be one of the writers who have made a permanent contribution to English literature.

In his *Forces in Modern British Literature* (1949), William York Tindall praises Wodehouse for his inimitable style, his amiability, and his hilarity. Tindall also notes that Wodehouse's treatment of the British upper classes is not satirical but protective, and that it was British Fascism that Wodehouse satirized.[34]

A. P. Ryan published a long review article in *The New Statesman* in 1953, in which he says that Wodehouse is wise to work in a very confined convention, since he can thereby give full scope to his genius for farcical situation, comic character, and wordplay. Ryan observes that the year of the first Bertie and Jeeves story is also the year of the Battle of the Somme. Working in a tradition that goes back to the macaronis, Wodehouse resurrected Bertie Wooster from the battlefield. Ryan also makes the interesting suggestion that Wodehouse modeled Jeeves on the housemasters of his youth, unruffled, unshocked, in control of their charges and patronizing them. And Ryan makes the more interesting, if less plausible, suggestion that if the mask of the comedian were to be stripped away, Wodehouse would turn out to be an aunt, not a Bertie Wooster.[35]

John W. Aldridge, in "P. G. Wodehouse: The Lesson of the Young Master," first published in *New World Writing* No. 13 (1958) and reprinted as the Introduction to *Selected Stories by P. G. Wodehouse* (1958) in The Modern Library, calls Wodehouse the most original writer of light social comedy in English, and also the most prolific and most popular. His books have been translated into all the major languages of Europe, and into Czech, Swedish, Polish, and Chinese. To explain why there is so little criticism of Wodehouse after so much time and so many books, Aldridge adduces several reasons. First, there is always a prejudice against writers of light comedy, a feeling that "entertainment" cannot have any literary value. Second, there is the problem of evaluating entertainment that is perfectly done. Third, and more important, Wodehouse has never needed the entree that criticism usually provides; and he has no equivalents to enable criticism to "exercise its comparative function." Last, great numbers of people were brought up on Wodehouse, or think that they were. Those who have actually read him when young do not read him again, or they read him with no new view. Those who imagine that they have read him never get around to reading him. In any case, such people simply take Wodehouse for granted.

Aldridge sees the Bertie and Jeeves books, together with the Blandings Castle books, as Wodehouse's greatest contribution to the art of fiction. Because, like all sagas, they carry a set of characters through a series of adventures, and because they are full of subplots, parallels, and cross-references, they give the reader the sense of moving in a world with its intimates and sharing the accretions of their experiences. So it is as one reads of the Glossops, Bingo Little, Sipperly, Bobbie Wickham, and so on. Aldridge finds the Bertie and Jeeves saga almost as complex as those of Balzac, Galsworthy, and Faulkner and, in its way, as satisfying.[36]

On October 13, 1961, two days before his eightieth birthday, *The Times Literary Supplement* printed an article on Wodehouse ("Mr. Wodehouse Carries On") that took up three-quarters of a page. Herbert Jenkins had published a new novel of Wodehouse's (*The Ice in the Bedroom*) and Richard Usborne's book, and had brought out the first twenty-five titles in a uniform edition of the works of Wodehouse (The Autograph Edition). In the new novel the writer of the article sees no loss of power. The dialogue is top-notch Wodehouse, and the complications of the plot are as skillfully managed as ever. Among the characters are several that have appeared in earlier novels—two young lovers, three American crooks, and the estate agent of Valley Fields, Mr. Cornelius—and a creation almost as magnificent as Aunt Dahlia, the bilge writer, Leila Yorke.

The *Times* critic thinks that Herbert Jenkins could have brought the volumes of The Uniform Edition out in a better order: first all of the Bertie and Jeeves books, then all of the Blandings Castle books, and so on. But the fact that the question of order should have arisen is significant. One does not wish to think of Wodehouse's work as an *oeuvre*, as though Wodehouse were Marcel Proust or one of the major Russian novelists; but the birthday, the beginnings of The Uniform Edition, and the extent of Wodehouse's total production rather compel one to. The problems presented to a reader who wishes to follow, for example, all the adventures of Bertie and Jeeves are considerable. (Bertie's and Jeeves's names are not in the titles of all the books in which they appear.) For such a reader, Mr. Usborne's book is as necessary as the Pleiade index is to a student of Proust.[37]

In 1962 *The Georgia Review* published an article by Clarke Olney called "Wodehouse and the Poets," an examination of Wodehouse's technique of quotation and allusion and of the sources on which he draws. Olney notes first of all that the nucleus of Wodehouse's extensive store consists of the "memory passages" that were part of the literary discipline of turn-of-the-century schools. Among the writers outside of the required ones are: Milton, Cowper, Burns, and Robert W. Service; among American poets Longfellow is the most frequently quoted, and then Whittier. Sometimes Wodehouse throws away a quotation, and sometimes he understates. Discovering his fiancée in the arms of another man, Lord Holbeton coughs and says, "I say." Wodehouse judges that the comment lacks fire and spirit; it is not the sort of thing that Othello would have said. He likes to ascribe quotations to incorrect and unlikely sources. In one of the golf stories James Baird, a champion of the time, is said to have remarked to J. H. Taylor, another great golfer, that certain shots seem, like a dome of many-colored glasses, to stain the white radiance of eternity. In Wodehouse's quotation and allusion, says Olney, there is more than mere fooling. The reader is challenged to spot the references, and when he does, he enjoys the shock of recognition. Moreover, the technique amounts to literary criticism, not only of bilge writers, but also of better ones.[38]

Literary histories, handbooks, and other works of reference should constitute an objective index of a writer's significance, though they cannot, in fact, be free of the subjective and even the eccentric. (*The Concise Encyclopedia of Modern World Literature*, published in 1963 under the editorship of Geoffrey Grigson, has a substantial entry on John Meade Falkner—and a good thing, too—but how many other reference books have anything at all on him?) Wodehouse's tally of reference works that include and those that exclude him is a respectable one. For instance, *A Literary History of England* (1948), edited by Albert C. Baugh, does not include him, though it makes brief mention of such writers as John Davys Beresford and Edward Frederick Benson. Edward Wagenknecht gives Wodehouse no place in his *Caval-*

cade of the English Novel (1945), not even in the Appendix, where he allows a third of a page to Rafael Sabatini and a full page to Forrest Reid. Donald Heiney's handbook *Contemporary Literature* (1954) leaves out Wodehouse.

But among the literary histories that include Wodehouse, *The Concise Cambridge History of English Literature* (1946), by George Sampson, has an enthusiastic paragraph on Wodehouse that is half as long as the one on Virginia Woolf. *The New Century Handbook of English Literature* (1956) edited by Clarence L. Barnhart, has an entry of more than a hundred words, a large part of it a good selective bibliography. In *A Dictionary of English Literature* (1945), by Homer A. Watt and William W. Watt, a volume in the Barnes and Noble "College Outline Series," there are a couple of hundred words on Wodehouse. In the third edition of *The Oxford Companion to English Literature* (1946) there are a hundred words. Cassell's *Encyclopedia of World Literature* (1954), edited by S. H. Steinberg, which runs from the beginnings of letters to the twentieth century and includes, together with literary history and literary movements, "a definitive gallery of the men and women who have written the world's great works," gives Wodehouse a hundred words, including bibliography.

The general encyclopedias have articles on Wodehouse, that in the 1961 edition of the *Britannica* running to about three hundred and fifty words. *The Penguin Dictionary of Quotations* (1962) has three from Wodehouse (but none of them at his best). Under "mixed metaphor" in their *Dictionary of American Usage* (1957), Bergan and Cornelia Evans refer to the bad metaphor used deliberately as a good joke, and cite, along with examples from Ring Lardner and the seventeenth-century Samuel Butler, one from Wodehouse: "The raspberry was not actually present, but he seemed to hear the beating of its wings."

If Wodehouse is a minor novelist, he has been an important influence on comic novelists of the twentieth century, some of whom are major figures beyond any question. Evelyn Waugh, for example, created a fictional world which, although differing vastly from Wodehouse's, still owes a great deal to it. In Waugh's novels causality is not suspended as it is in Wodehouse's. Waugh's moral system is rigidly real, and people pay for their ignorance and folly as they do in the world of fact. But some of the plots of Waugh could be switched for some of those in Wodehouse, and nobody would be the worse. Like Wodehouse, Waugh makes much use of mistakes in identity and masquerades, coincidences and outside chances and arbitrary disasters. In *Vile Bodies* (1928) Agatha Runcible (a name worthy of Wodehouse, though the surname is, of course, derived from Edward Lear) is thought by British customs officials to be an international jewel thief; to her great indignation, she is frisked and stripped.

On a wild bet Adam Fenwick-Symes, the hero of *Vile Bodies,* wins a thousand pounds, which is instantly appropriated by a drunk major. Nina Blount and Adam spend Christmas with Nina's father, Colonel Blount, who thinks that Adam is Nina's husband, Eddy Littlejohn. Delighted to receive a large check from the Colonel, Adam later discovers that it is signed "Charlie Chaplin." (Like Freddie Threepwood, the Colonel is a passionate devotee of the movies.) In *Scoop* (1938) William Boot, a mild writer of a nature column, is sent out as foreign correspondent by an editor who thinks that he is another writer of the same name. In *Decline and Fall* (1928) Paul Pennyfeather, in Blackstone Gaol, discovers that Philbrick, the butler at his old school, is a trusty, and that Mr. Prendergast, another schoolmaster, is the chaplain. In *Put Out More Flags* (1942) Basil Seal lies, bluffs, blackmails, and wangles his way through the Ministry of Information and his job as an evacuation officer.

There are also resemblances between types and single characters in Waugh and those in Wodehouse. The rogue Grimes in *Decline and Fall* is not unlike the rogue Ukridge, and he describes his misadventures in a favorite phrase of Wodehouse's: "in the soup." The absent-minded Colonel Blount is like the absent-minded Lord Emsworth, and his country house, Doubting, is like Blandings, with the difference that is implied in the names. The Bright Young People are as silly as the Eggs, Beans, and Crumpets of Wodehouse, but without access to a Jeeves. As regards style, Waugh himself, in an interview about his work, said that the great writers of the nineteenth century influenced him indirectly (he called them his "education"), but that Wodehouse influenced his style directly.[39]

Perhaps Anthony Powell, especially in the five novels that he wrote before he embarked on *The Music of Time* series, has been as much influenced by Wodehouse as Evelyn Waugh was, though again there is, of course, a seriousness that is absent in Wodehouse. The very titles of Powell's early novels, to say nothing of the epigraphs, taken from such sources as Burton's *Anatomy of Melancholy* and the sermons of John Wesley, point to their serious side. The air of the English countryside in Powell's *From a View to a Death* (1933) is charged with something very different from the innocence of Wodehouse. The obsessions of the characters are neurotic, the entanglements are sinister, and the farce is literally fatal. Still, the silly young men and women, the eccentric squires, and the village types of *From a View to a Death* have much in common with those who constitute an important part of Wodehouse's stock in trade. In *Venusberg* (1932) Lushington and De Costa, the one trying to conceal his nervousness and shyness by creeping about rooms pretending that he is not really there, the other by shouting and laughing and upsetting things, are not far from the dolts who forgather at the Drones Club. And Blore-Smith, the hero of *Agents and Patients* (1936), fairly rich and unusually stupid, obligingly paying out large sums of money—simply asking to be exploited by people with more brains and fewer scruples—is a Bertie without a Jeeves.

However different their attitudes and purposes, younger writers like Kingsley Amis and John Wain owe much to the techniques of farce which Wodehouse developed and with which he has operated for so many years. Indeed, Wodehouse has influenced English comic novelists who have just published their first or second book, and one such writer may well have the last word. Discussing his own work in a recent interview, Auberon Waugh said that he supposed he made jokes like those of his father and P. G. Wodehouse. Then he remarked that all English comic writers are so much influenced by Wodehouse that they must constantly try *not* to write Wodehouse's kind of comedy, in order that they may write their own.[40]

Notes and References

Most of the references to Wodehouse's books are, as will be seen, to the uniform edition (The Autograph Edition), published by Herbert Jenkins, Ltd., London. Dates of original publication are given in the text and in the bibliography.

Preface

1. My friend Felix Stefanile has given me the list of Wodehouse novels in one Italian bookseller's catalogue. Altogether there are thirty-six titles; among them are *Avanti, Jeeves; Grazie, Jeeves; Le Serate di Mulliner; Jill, Ragazza Bizzarra; Parla Mister Mulliner; Sam il Dinamico.*

Chapter One

1. Wodehouse himself is the source of most of the biographical information. *Performing Flea* (London, 1953; under title *Author! Author!*, New York, 1962) is a collection of letters from Wodehouse to William Townend, with comments and additional material by Townend. It is the most important of the biographical sources. *America, I Like You* (New York, 1956; under title *Over Seventy*, London, 1957) is a collection of autobiographical essays with digressions, the digressions taking up more space than the autobiography. *Bring on the Girls* (New York, 1953; London, 1954), written in collaboration with Guy Bolton, is a book about Wodehouse's work in musical comedy. "Berlin Broadcasts," *Encounter*, III, 4 (October, 1954), pp. 17–24, and *Encounter*, III, 5 (November 1954), pp. 39–47, are the texts of the broadcasts that Wodehouse made over the German radio. Richard Usborne's *Wodehouse at Work* (London, 1961) is very useful, especially for Wodehouse's family, school years, and early career. Malcolm Muggeridge's "The Wodehouse Affair," *The New Statesman*, LXII (August 4, 1961), pp. 50–51, is an account of Wodehouse during World War II. Harry Flannery's *Assignment to Berlin* (New York, 1942) includes material on Wodehouse at the same period. Muggeridge is sympathetic, and Flannery is not.

2. *Over Seventy* (London, 1957), p. 54.

3. *Ibid.*, p. 53.

4. The philosopher was G. E. Moore, and the explorer was Sir Ernest Shackleton.

5. Later published as two novels, the first half as *Mike at Wrykyn,* the second as *Enter Psmith* and also as *Mike and Psmith.*

6. *Mike and Psmith* (London, 1953), p. 45.

7. *The Head of Kay's* (London, 1905), pp. 254–55.

8. *Something Fresh* (London, 1915), p. 13.

9. Unfortunately for Wodehouse, the Adlon was the original "Grand Hotel," the model and symbol of luxurious hotels all over the world. Escoffier invented *sauce diable* there, and Kaiser Wilhelm was a patron. John Gunther considered it to be the most splendid hotel that he had ever stayed in. During World War II it was, of course, less splendid. Now in the Soviet Sector of Berlin, it has declined out of recognition. See Gunther's *Inside Europe Today* (Revised Edition, New York, 1962), p. 64.

10. *Performing Flea* (London, 1953), p. 110.

11. *Ibid.*, p. 109.

12. Malcolm Muggeridge, "The Wodehouse Affair," *The New Statesman,* 62 (August 4, 1961), p. 50.

13. *Encounter,* III, 4 (October, 1954), p. 18.

14. *Ibid.*

15. *Dickens, Dali and Others* (New York, 1946), p. 228.

16. *Assignment to Berlin* (New York, 1942), p. 351.

17. *Ibid.*, p. 350.

18. *Ibid.*, p. 346.

19. *Time,* LXXVIII, 4 (July 28, 1961), p. 20.

20. *Performing Flea,* p. 121.

Chapter Two

1. Wodehouse wrote seven public school books (the division of *Mike* into two novels makes eight volumes). *Tales of St. Austin's* is a collection of short stories; all the other public school volumes are novels. *The Little Nugget* has a preparatory school as one of its backgrounds, and a schoolboy as a major character, but it is one of the light romances, not a preparatory school novel. *William Tell Told Again* is a children's book. In England a "public school" is traditionally one independently financed. Boys attend preparatory schools from about seven to thirteen and public schools from about thirteen to eighteen.

2. George Orwell, "Boys' Weeklies," *Dickens, Dali and Others* (New York, 1946), pp. 95–96.

3. *A Prefect's Uncle* (London, 1924), p. 3.

4. *Ibid.*, p. 29.

5. *Mike at Wrykyn* (London, 1953), p. 55.

6. *The Head of Kay's* (London, 1922), p. 224.

7. *The Gold Bat* (London, 1933), p. 20.

8. *Mike at Wrykyn*, p. 21.

9. *Ibid.*, p. 130.

10. *The Pothunters* (London, 1902), p. 32.

11. *The Gold Bat*, p. 16.

12. *The Head of Kay's*, p. 20.

13. The trick is also popular at the more serious Sedleigh.

14. *Mike and Psmith* (London, 1953), p. 58.

15. *Mike at Wrykyn*, p. 24.

16. *The Pothunters*, p. 174.

17. *Mike at Wrykyn*, p. 189.

18. Anthony Powell, "The Wat'ry Glade," *The Old School*, ed. by Graham Greene (London, 1934), pp. 147–48.

19. *A Prefect's Uncle*, p. 205.

20. *Ibid.*, pp. 114–15.

21. *The Head of Kay's*, p. 1.

22. *Mike and Psmith*, p. 18.

23. Richard Usborne, *Wodehouse at Work* (London, 1961), p. 53.

24. *The Gold Bat*, p. 144.

25. *Mike and Psmith*, p. 9.

26. *The Pothunters*, p. 178.

Chapter Three

1. *Love Among the Chickens* (The Autograph Edition, London, 1921), p. 165.

2. *Ibid.*, pp. 172–73. In this passage Garnet is at the same time apologizing for himself, kidding the serious novel, and parodying the kind of novel that he writes. Such passages are the beginnings of Wodehouse's later parodies of romantic literature.

3. *Ibid.*, p. 94–95.

4. *Ibid.*, p. 184.

5. *Ibid.*, p. 190.

6. Richard Usborne, *Wodehouse at Work* (London, 1961), p. 81. Usborne observes, for instance, that Cullingworth calls everyone "laddie," has an adoring, victimized little wife, is chronically broke, and is beset by creditors.

7. *Love Among the Chickens*, p. 53.

8. *Ibid.*, p. 123. Tennyson's lines about kind hearts and coronets are among Wodehouse's favorites. In one form or another, they appear dozens of times over the next sixty years.

9. *Ibid.*, p. 150.

10. *Psmith in the City* (London, 1950), p. 259.

11. *Ibid.*, p. 27.

12. *Ibid.*, p. 111.

13. Usborne, *Wodehouse at Work*, p. 64.

14. *Mike and Psmith* (London, 1953), p. 174.

15. *Psmith in the City*, p. 143.

16. *Ibid.*, p. 130.

17. *Ibid.*, p. 111.

18. *Ibid.*, p. 248.

19. *Psmith Journalist* is a reworking of an earlier novel, *The Prince and Betty* (London, 1912).

20. *Psmith Journalist* (London, 1950), p. 13.

21. *Ibid.*, p. 12.

22. *Ibid.*, v. When Wodehouse goes on to make the incredible statement that most of the events in the story are based on actual ones, he must have the gunplay and the gangsters in mind. He appears to believe that for every murder reported in the papers there are scores of unreported ones.

23. *Ibid.*, p. 82.

24. *Ibid.*, p. 38.

25. *Ibid.*, p. 91.

26. *Ibid.*, p. 33.

27. *Psmith in the City*, p. 144.

28. Usborne, *Wodehouse at Work*, p. 71. Among the sources of Psmith's speech, Usborne notices the Sherlock Holmes stories, Anstey's *Vice Versa* and *Baboo Jabberjee*, and Dickens' Dick Swiveller.

29. *Mike and Psmith*, p. 155.

Chapter Four

1. *Summer Moonshine* (The Autograph Edition, London, 1956), p. 185.

2. *Hot Water* (The Autograph Edition, London, 1956), p. 222.

3. *Something Fresh* (London, 1915), pp. 101–2.

4. *Ibid.*, p. 3.

5. *A Gentleman of Leisure* (The Autograph Edition, London, 1962), p. 90.

6. *A Damsel in Distress* (The Autograph Edition, London, 1956), p. 33. Upon his arrival at Sedleigh, Psmith appropriates a choice study from the boy who occupied it the previous year.

7. *Psmith in the City* (London, 1950), p. 264.

8. *Leave It to Psmith* (The Autograph Edition, London, 1961), p. 264.

9. *Summer Moonshine,* p. 141.

10. *Quick Service* (The Autograph Edition, London, 1960), p. 133.

11. *Something Fresh,* p. 171.

12. *Quick Service,* p. 132.

13. *Jill the Reckless* (The Autograph Edition, London, 1958), p. 184.

14. *Ibid.,* p. 293.

15. *Hot Water,* p. 89.

16. *A Damsel in Distress,* pp. 22–23.

17. *Ibid.,* p. 144.

18. *Quick Service,* p. 129.

19. *The Girl on the Boat* (The Autograph Edition, London, 1956), p. 58.

20. *Ibid.,* p. 55.

Chapter Five

1. *Carry On, Jeeves* (The Autograph Edition, London, 1960), p. 105.

2. *The Luck of the Bodkins* (The Autograph Edition, London, 1956), p. 27.

3. *Ibid.,* p. 29.

4. *Carry On, Jeeves,* p. 168.

5. *The Code of the Woosters* (The Autograph Edition, London, 1962), p. 12.

6. *Thank You, Jeeves* (The Autograph Edition, London, 1956), p. 9.

7. For example, Stephanie Byng is usually called Stiffy; Roberta Wickham, Bobbie; Cora Pirbright, Corky.

8. *Jeeves in the Offing* (London, 1960), p. 13.

9. Richard Usborne, *Wodehouse at Work* (London, 1961), p. 130.

10. *The Code of the Woosters* (The Autograph Edition, London, 1962), p. 83.

11. *Jeeves in the Offing,* p. 39.

12. *Thank You, Jeeves,* p. 15.

13. *Jeeves in the Offing,* p. 22.

14. *Carry On, Jeeves,* p. 139.

15. *Thank You, Jeeves,* p. 106.

16. *Carry On, Jeeves,* p. 181.

17. *The Code of the Woosters,* p. 214.

18. *Leave It to Psmith* (The Autograph Edition, London, 1961), p. 10.

19. *Meet Mr. Mulliner* (The Autograph Edition, London, 1956), p. 40.

20. *Ibid.,* p. 51.

21. *Hot Water* (The Autograph Edition, London, 1956), p. 69.
22. *Thank You, Jeeves*, p. 10.
23. *Jeeves in the Offing*, p. 82.
24. *The Code of the Woosters*, p. 115.
25. *Stiff Upper Lip, Jeeves* (London, 1963), p. 73.
26. *The Code of the Woosters*, p. 111.
27. *Thank You, Jeeves*, p. 132.
28. Eric Bentley, ed., *Let's Get a Divorce!* (New York, 1958), p. vii.
29. *The Mating Season* (London, 1949), p. 166.
30. *The Clicking of Cuthbert* (The Autograph Edition, London, 1956), p. 50.
31. *The Mating Season*, p. 217.
32. *Jeeves in the Offing*, pp. 183–84.
33. *Ibid.*, p. 148.
34. *Thank You, Jeeves*, pp. 10–11.
35. *Meet Mr. Mulliner*, p. 127.
36. *The Heart of a Goof* (The Autograph Edition, London, 1956), p. 33.

Chapter Six

1. *Something Fresh* (London, 1915), p. 82.
2. *The Prince and Betty* (New York, 1912), p. 10.
3. *The Coming of Bill* (London, n.d.), p. 60.
4. *The Prince and Betty*, p. 108.
5. *Uncle Dynamite* (London, 1948), p. 240.
6. *Stiff Upper Lip, Jeeves* (London, 1963), p. 128.
7. *The Code of the Woosters* (The Autograph Edition, London, 1962), p. 107.
8. *Performing Flea* (London, 1953), p. 85.
9. *Something Fresh*, pp. 38–39.
10. *Blandings Castle* (The Autograph Edition, London, 1957), p. 177.
11. *Jill the Reckless* (The Autograph Edition, London, 1958), p. 219.
12. *The Coming of Bill*, p. 107.
13. *Jeeves in the Offing* (The Autograph Edition, London, 1960), p. 108.
14. *The Mating Season* (London, 1949), p. 114.
15. *The Luck of the Bodkins* (The Autograph Edition, London, 1956), p. 33.
16. *Bertie Wooster Sees It Through* (New York, 1955), p. 15.
17. *Ibid.*, p. 9.
18. *Jeeves in the Offing*, p. 139.

19. *The Clicking of Cuthbert* (The Autograph Edition, London, 1956), p. 21.

20. *A Damsel in Distress* (The Autograph Edition, London, 1956), p. 64.

21. *Something Fresh*, p. 127.

22. *The Girl on the Boat* (The Autograph Edition, London, 1956), p. 113.

23. *Performing Flea*, pp. 38–39.

24. *Summer Moonshine* (The Autograph Edition, London, 1956), p. 16.

25. *Mike and Psmith* (London, 1953), p. 20.

26. *If I Were You* (The Autograph Edition, London, 1958), p. 21.

27. *A Damsel in Distress*, p. 30.

28. *Meet Mr. Mulliner* (The Autograph Edition, London, 1956), p. 32.

29. *A Damsel in Distress*, p. 165.

30. *Uncle Dynamite*, p. 80.

Chapter Seven

1. Lionel Stevenson, "The Antecedents of P. G. Wodehouse," *Arizona Quarterly*, V (Autumn, 1949), pp. 226–34.

2. Byron's Don Juan, Stevenson notes, does not fit the tradition because he has too much vigor, both physical and emotional.

3. *Leave It to Psmith* (The Autograph Edition, London, 1961), p. 27.

4. Quoted in Virginia Woolf, *The Common Reader: Second Series* (London, 1932), p. 151.

5. *Performing Flea* (London, 1953), p. 105.

6. *If I Were You* (The Autograph Edition, London, 1958), p. 147.

7. *Ibid.*, p. 55.

8. *The Pothunters* (London, 1902), p. 158.

9. One might think that the figure of the hen-pecked bishop derived from Trollope, but Wodehouse did not read Trollope until later.

10. *Meet Mr. Mulliner* (The Autograph Edition, London, 1956), pp. 58–59.

11. *Ibid.*, p. 155.

12. *Ibid.*, p. 30.

13. *Psmith in the City* (London, 1950), pp. 25–26.

14. *A Few Quick Ones* (New York, 1959), p. 147 and p. 139.

15. *The Luck of the Bodkins* (The Autograph Edition, London, 1956), p. 150.

16. *Quick Service* (The Autograph Edition, London, 1960), p. 61.

17. *The Code of the Woosters* (The Autograph Edition, London, 1962), p. 33.

18. *Quick Service*, p. 23.

19. *Ibid.*, p. 86.

20. *A Few Quick Ones*, p. 191.

21. *Carry On, Jeeves* (The Autograph Edition, London, 1960), p. 7.

22. *A Few Quick Ones*, p. 82.

23. *Quick Service*, p. 40.

24. *Over Seventy* (London, 1957), p. 189.

25. Richard Usborne saw the typescript of *Jeeves in the Offing* and the pencilled notes at Sotheby's, among other manuscripts to be sold for charity. A New York dealer paid one hundred guineas for the typescript and the notes.

26. The story might be true at that. Ezra Pound is said to have pinned the pages of manuscripts to strings running up and down the room, and to have walked about rereading and revising.

27. *Performing Flea*, p. 128.

28. Richard Usborne, *Wodehouse at Work* (London, 1961).

29. Frank Swinnerton, *The Georgian Scene* (Sixth Edition, New York, 1951), pp. 368–71.

30. *Tales of St. Austin's* (London, 1903), p. 55.

31. John Hayward, "P. G. Wodehouse," *The Saturday Book*, 1941–1942 (London, 1942), pp. 372–79.

32. George Orwell, "In Defense of P. G. Wodehouse," *Dickens, Dali and Others* (New York, 1946), pp. 222–43.

33. John Lardner, "Wodehouse, Past and Present," *The New Yorker*, XXIV (May 22, 1948), pp. 111–13.

34. Lionel Stevenson, "The Antecedents of P. G. Wodehouse," *Arizona Quarterly*, V (Autumn, 1949), p. 234; William York Tindall, *Forces in Modern British Literature* (New York, 1949), pp. 137–38.

35. A. P. Ryan, "Wooster's Progress," *The New Statesman*, XLV (June 20, 1953), p. 737.

36. John W. Aldridge, "P. G. Wodehouse: The Lesson of the Young Master," *Selected Stories by P. G. Wodehouse* (New York, 1958), pp. xi–xxv.

37. *The Times Literary Supplement*, No. 3111 (October 13, 1961), p. 682.

38. Clarke Olney, "Wodehouse and the Poets," *The Georgia Review*, XVI (Winter, 1962), pp. 392–99.

39. "The Art of Fiction XXX, Evelyn Waugh," *Paris Review*, XXX (Summer–Fall, 1963), p. 80.

40. *New York Times Book Review*, LXIX (July 19, 1964), p. 22.

Selected Bibliography

Most of Wodehouse's books have been published in both England and the United States, and most have gone through several editions. The Bibliography includes publishers and dates of first editions, variant titles, and dates of titles in The Autograph Edition so far.

PRIMARY SOURCES

The Pothunters. London: A. and C. Black, 1902.

A Prefect's Uncle. London: A. and C. Black, 1903.

Tales of St. Austin's. London: A. and C. Black, 1903.

The Gold Bat. London: A. and C. Black, 1904.

William Tell Told Again. London: A. and C. Black, 1904.

The Head of Kay's. London: A. and C. Black, 1905.

Love Among the Chickens. London: George Newnes, 1906. Autograph Edition, 1963.

The White Feather. London: A. and C. Black, 1907.

Not George Washington (with Herbert Westbrook). London: Cassell, 1907.

By the Way Book (with Herbert Westbrook). London: Globe, 1908.

The Swoop. London: Alston Rivers, 1909.

Mike. London: A. and C. Black, 1909.

Psmith in the City. London: A. and C. Black, 1910.

A Gentleman of Leisure. London: Alston Rivers, 1910; under the title *The Intrusion of Jimmy*, New York: W. J. Watt and Company, 1910. Autograph Edition, under former title, 1962.

The Prince and Betty. London: George Newnes, 1912; New York: W. J. Watt and Company, 1912.

The Little Nugget. London: Methuen, 1913; New York: W. J. Watt and Company, 1914.

The Man Upstairs. London: Methuen, 1914.

Something Fresh. London: Methuen, 1915; under the title *Something New*, New York: D. Appleton and Company, 1915.

Psmith Journalist. London: A. and C. Black, 1915.

Uneasy Money. New York: D. Appleton and Company, 1916; London: Methuen, 1917.

The Man with Two Left Feet. London: Methuen, 1917.

Piccadilly Jim. New York: Dodd, Mead and Company, 1917; London: Herbert Jenkins, 1918.

My Man Jeeves. London: George Newnes, 1919.

A Damsel in Distress. London: Herbert Jenkins, 1919; New York: George H. Doran Company, 1919. Autograph Edition, 1956.

Their Mutual Child. New York: Boni and Liveright, 1919; under the title *The Coming of Bill,* London: Herbert Jenkins, 1920.

The Indiscretions of Archie. London: Herbert Jenkins, 1921; New York: George H. Doran Company, 1921. Autograph Edition, 1965.

The Little Warrior. New York: George H. Doran Company, 1920; under the title *Jill the Reckless,* London: Herbert Jenkins, 1921. Autograph Edition, under latter title, 1958.

The Clicking of Cuthbert. London: Herbert Jenkins, 1922; under the title *Golf without Tears,* New York: George H. Doran Company, 1924. Autograph Edition, under former title, 1956.

The Girl on the Boat. London: Herbert Jenkins, 1922; under the title *Three Men and a Maid,* New York: George H. Doran Company, 1922. Autograph Edition, under former title, 1956.

The Adventures of Sally. London: Herbert Jenkins, 1922; under the title *Mostly Sally,* New York: George H. Doran Company, 1923.

The Inimitable Jeeves. London: Herbert Jenkins, 1923; under the title *Jeeves,* New York: George H. Doran Company, 1923. Autograph Edition, under former title, 1956.

Leave It to Psmith. London: Herbert Jenkins, 1923; New York: George H. Doran Company, 1924. Autograph Edition, 1961.

Ukridge. London: Herbert Jenkins, 1924; under the title *He Rather Enjoyed It,* New York: George H. Doran Company, 1925. Autograph Edition, under former title, 1960.

Bill the Conqueror. London: Methuen, 1924; New York: George H. Doran Company, 1924.

Carry On, Jeeves (a reissue of *My Man Jeeves*). London: Herbert Jenkins, 1925; New York: George H. Doran Company, 1927. Autograph Edition, 1960.

Sam the Sudden. London: Methuen, 1925; under the title *Sam in the Suburbs,* New York: George H. Doran Company, 1925.

The Heart of a Goof. London: Herbert Jenkins, 1926; under the title *Divots,* New York: George H. Doran Company, 1927. Autograph Edition, under former title, 1956.

The Small Bachelor. London: Methuen, 1927; New York: George H. Doran Company, 1927.

Selected Bibliography

Meet Mr. Mulliner. London: Herbert Jenkins, 1927; Garden City, New York: Doubleday, Doran and Company, 1928. Autograph Edition, 1956.

Money for Nothing. London: Herbert Jenkins, 1928; Garden City, New York: Doubleday, Doran and Company, 1928. Autograph Edition, 1959.

Mr. Mulliner Speaking. London: Herbert Jenkins, 1929. Autograph Edition, 1961.

Summer Lightning. London: Herbert Jenkins, 1929; under the title *Fish Preferred,* Garden City, New York: Doubleday, Doran and Company, 1929. Autograph Edition, under former title, 1964.

Very Good, Jeeves. London: Herbert Jenkins, 1930; Garden City, New York: Doubleday, Doran and Company, 1930. Autograph Edition, 1958.

Big Money. London: Herbert Jenkins, 1931; Garden City, New York: Doubleday, Doran and Company, 1931. Autograph Edition, 1965.

If I Were You. London: Herbert Jenkins, 1931; Garden City, New York: Doubleday, Doran and Company, 1931. Autograph Edition, 1958.

Doctor Sally. London: Methuen, 1932.

Hot Water. London: Herbert Jenkins, 1932; Garden City, New York: Doubleday, Doran and Company, 1932. Autograph Edition, 1956.

Louder and Funnier. London: Faber and Faber, 1932. Autograph Edition, 1963.

Mulliner Nights. London: Herbert Jenkins, 1933; Garden City, New York: Doubleday, Doran and Company, 1933. Autograph Edition, 1966.

Heavy Weather. London: Herbert Jenkins, 1933; Boston: Little, Brown and Company, 1933. Autograph Edition, 1960.

Thank You, Jeeves. London: Herbert Jenkins, 1934; Boston: Little, Brown and Company, 1934. Autograph Edition, 1956.

Right Ho, Jeeves. London: Herbert Jenkins, 1934; under the title *Brinkley Manor,* Boston: Little, Brown and Company, 1934. Autograph Edition, under former title, 1957.

Enter Psmith (the second half of *Mike* published as a separate volume). London: A. and C. Black, 1935; New York: The Macmillan Company, 1935.

Blandings Castle. London: Herbert Jenkins, 1935; Garden City, New York: Doubleday, Doran and Company, 1935. Autograph Edition, 1957.

The Luck of the Bodkins. London: Herbert Jenkins, 1935; Boston: Little, Brown and Company, 1936. Autograph Edition, 1956.

Young Men in Spats. London: Herbert Jenkins, 1936; Garden City,

New York: Doubleday, Doran and Company, 1936. Autograph Edition, 1957.

Laughing Gas. London: Herbert Jenkins, 1936; Garden City, New York: Doubleday, Doran and Company, 1936. Autograph Edition, 1959.

Lord Emsworth and Others. London: Herbert Jenkins, 1937; under the title *The Crime Wave at Blandings,* Garden City, New York: Doubleday, Doran and Company, 1937. Autograph Edition, under former title, 1956.

Summer Moonshine. Garden City, New York: Doubleday, Doran and Company, 1937; London: Herbert Jenkins, 1938. Autograph Edition, 1956.

The Code of the Woosters. London: Herbert Jenkins, 1938; Garden City, New York: Doubleday, Doran and Company, 1938. Autograph Edition, 1962.

Uncle Fred in the Springtime. London: Herbert Jenkins, 1939; Garden City, New York: Doubleday, Doran and Company, 1939. Autograph Edition, 1962.

Eggs, Beans and Crumpets. London: Herbert Jenkins, 1940; Garden City, New York: Doubleday, Doran and Company, 1940. Autograph Edition, 1963.

Quick Service. London: Herbert Jenkins, 1940; Garden City, New York: Doubleday, Doran and Company, 1940. Autograph Edition, 1960.

Money in the Bank. Garden City, New York: Doubleday, Doran and Company, 1942; London: Herbert Jenkins, 1946.

Joy in the Morning. Garden City, New York: Doubleday, Doran and Company, 1946; London: Herbert Jenkins, 1947.

Full Moon. London: Herbert Jenkins, 1947; Garden City, New York: Doubleday, Doran and Company, 1947.

Spring Fever. London: Herbert Jenkins, 1948.

Uncle Dynamite. London: Herbert Jenkins, 1948.

The Mating Season. London: Herbert Jenkins, 1949.

Nothing Serious. London: Herbert Jenkins, 1950; Garden City, New York: Doubleday, Doran and Company, 1951. Autograph Edition, 1964.

The Old Reliable. London: Herbert Jenkins, 1951; Garden City, New York: Doubleday, Doran and Company, 1951.

Barmy in Wonderland. London: Herbert Jenkins, 1952; under the title *Angel Cake,* Garden City, New York: Doubleday, Doran and Company, 1952. Autograph Edition, under former title, 1958.

Pigs Have Wings. London: Herbert Jenkins, 1952; Garden City, New York: Doubleday, Doran and Company, 1952.

Selected Bibliography

Mike at Wrykyn (the first half of *Mike* published as a separate volume). London: Herbert Jenkins, 1953.

Mike and Psmith (the second half of *Mike* published as a separate volume). London: Herbert Jenkins, 1953.

Ring for Jeeves. London: Herbert Jenkins, 1953; under the title *The Return of Jeeves*, New York: Simon and Schuster, 1954. Autograph Edition, under former title, 1963.

Performing Flea. London: Herbert Jenkins, 1953; under the title *Author! Author!*, New York: Simon and Schuster, 1962.

Bring on the Girls (with Guy Bolton). New York: Simon and Schuster, 1953; London: Herbert Jenkins, 1954.

Jeeves and the Feudal Spirit. London: Herbert Jenkins, 1954. Autograph Edition, 1966.

Bertie Wooster Sees It Through. New York: Simon and Schuster, 1955.

America, I Like You. New York: Simon and Schuster, 1956; under the title *Over Seventy*, London: Herbert Jenkins, 1957.

French Leave. London: Herbert Jenkins, 1956; New York: Simon and Schuster, 1959.

Something Fishy. London: Herbert Jenkins, 1957; under the title *The Butler Did It*, New York: Simon and Schuster, 1957.

Cocktail Time. London: Herbert Jenkins, 1958; New York: Simon and Schuster, 1958.

A Few Quick Ones. London: Herbert Jenkins, 1959; New York: Simon and Schuster, 1959.

Jeeves in the Offing. London: Herbert Jenkins, 1960; under the title *How Right You Are, Jeeves*, New York: Simon and Schuster, 1960.

Ice in the Bedroom. London: Herbert Jenkins, 1961; New York: Simon and Schuster, 1961.

Service with a Smile. New York: Simon and Schuster, 1961; London: Herbert Jenkins, 1962.

Stiff Upper Lip, Jeeves. London: Herbert Jenkins, 1963; New York: Simon and Schuster, 1963.

Frozen Assets. London: Herbert Jenkins, 1964; under the title *Biffen's Millions*, New York: Simon and Schuster, 1964.

The Brinkmanship of Galahad Threepwood. New York: Simon and Schuster, 1965; under the title *Galahad at Blandings*, London: Herbert Jenkins, 1965.

Selections

The Jeeves Omnibus. London: Herbert Jenkins, 1931.

Nothing But Wodehouse. Ed. by Ogden Nash. Garden City, New York: Doubleday, Doran and Company, 1932.

P. G. Wodehouse. London: Methuen, 1934. (Methuen's Library of Humor.)

The Mulliner Omnibus. London: Herbert Jenkins, 1935.

The Week-End Wodehouse. London: Herbert Jenkins, 1939; Garden City, New York: Doubleday, Doran and Company, 1939.

Wodehouse on Golf. Garden City, New York: Doubleday, Doran and Company, 1940.

Selected Stories by P. G. Wodehouse. Ed. with an introduction by John W. Aldridge. New York: Random House, 1958. (The Modern Library.)

The Most of P. G. Wodehouse. New York: Simon and Schuster, 1960.

SECONDARY SOURCES

ALDRIDGE, JOHN W. "P. G. Wodehouse: The Lesson of the Young Master." *New World Writing* No.13. New York: New American Library, 1958. Reprinted as Introduction to *Selected Stories by P. G. Wodehouse.* New York: Random House, 1958, pp. xi–xxv. (The Modern Library.) Considers Wodehouse to be the best writer of light comedy in the twentieth century, and the Bertie and Jeeves stories and novels to be the best of his work.

HAYWARD, JOHN. "P. G. Wodehouse." *The Saturday Book,* 1941–1942. London: Hutchinson, 1941. Shows how much the material for the later books is present in the earlier ones. Includes biographical information.

LARDNER, JOHN. "Wodehouse Past and Present." *The New Yorker,* XXIV (May 22, 1948), 111–13. Believes that Wodehouse's current work is not up to his past work, but that Wodehouse is a "great verbal comedian," a writer who can make one laugh out loud.

OLNEY, CLARKE. "Wodehouse and the Poets." *The Georgia Review,* XVI, 4 (Winter, 1962), 392–99. Discusses the sources of Wodehouse's quotations and the ways in which he uses them. Suggests that the technique is sometimes a form of literary criticism.

ORWELL, GEORGE. "In Defense of P. G. Wodehouse." *Dickens, Dali and Others.* New York: Reynal and Hitchcock, 1946. Notes that the atmosphere of Wodehouse's novels has not changed since 1925 and that the best known characters appeared before that date. Points out the importance of the public school code.

RYAN, A. P. "Wooster's Progress." *The New Statesman,* XLV (June 20, 1953), 737. Says Wodehouse is wise to work in a confined convention that suits his comic genius perfectly. Suggests that Jeeves is modeled on housemasters at Dulwich.

STEVENSON, LIONEL. "The Antecedents of P. G. Wodehouse." *Arizona*

Quarterly, V (Autumn, 1959), 226–34. Points to equivalents to Wodehouse in comic writers from Jonson to Wilde. Says that Wodehouse, having created characters familiar to the whole reading public, has made a permanent contribution to English literature.

SWINNERTON, FRANK. *The Georgian Literary Scene*. 6th Edition. New York: Farrar and Strauss, 1951. Has praise for Wodehouse as contriver of comic episodes, but greater praise for Wodehouse as inventor of comic language.

USBORNE, RICHARD. *Wodehouse at Work*. London: Herbert Jenkins, 1961. Organizes discussion of whole body of Wodehouse's work by characters and cycles. Has information on Wodehouse's early years. Valuable appendices.

VOORHEES, RICHARD J. "The Jolly Old World of P. G. Wodehouse." *The South Atlantic Quarterly*, LXI, 2 (Spring, 1962) 213–22. Discusses the innocence and unreality of Wodehouse's world, and the attractions for Wodehouse in both the aristocratic and the democratic traditions.

Index

Index

Index